Pablo Picasso

Pablo Picasso

John W. Selfridge

CHELSEA HOUSE PUBLISHERS
NEW YORK ■ PHILADELPHIA

CHELSEA HOUSE PUBLISHERS

Editorial Director: Richard Rennert
Executive Managing Editor: Karyn Gullen Browne
Executive Editor: Sean Dolan
Picture Editor: Adrian G. Allen
Art Director: Robert Mitchell
Manufacturing Director: Gerald Levine
Production Coordinator: Marie Claire Cebrián-Ume

HISPANICS OF ACHIEVEMENT
Senior Editor: Philip Koslow

Staff for PABLO PICASSO
Associate Editor: David Carter
Copy Editor: Nicole Greenblatt
Designer: M. Cambraia Magalhaes
Picture Research: Patricia Burns
Cover Illustration: Bradford Brown

3 5 7 9 8 6 4

Library of Congress Cataloging-in-Publication Data
Selfridge, John W.
Pablo Picasso/John W. Selfridge.
p. cm.—(Hispanics of achievement)
Includes bibliographical references and index.
Summary: Discusses the life and work of the well-known twentieth-century painter, describing how his art was influenced by the events in Spain and his early years there.
ISBN 0-7910-1777-X
0-7910-1996-9 (pbk.)
1. Picasso, Pablo, 1881–1973—Juvenile literature. 2. Painters—France—Biography—Juvenile literature. [1. Picasso, Pablo, 1881–1973. 2. Artists.] I. Title. II. Series.
93-19205
ND553.P5S3997 1993
CIP
759.4—dc20
[B]
AC

CONTENTS

HISPANICS OF ACHIEVEMENT

JOAN BAEZ
Mexican-American folksinger

RUBÉN BLADES
Panamanian lawyer and entertainer

JORGE LUIS BORGES
Argentine writer

PABLO CASALS
Spanish cellist and conductor

MIGUEL DE CERVANTES
Spanish writer

CESAR CHAVEZ
Mexican-American labor leader

JULIO CÉSAR CHÁVEZ
Mexican boxing champion

EL CID
Spanish military leader

HENRY CISNEROS
Mexican-American political leader

ROBERTO CLEMENTE
Puerto Rican baseball player

SALVADOR DALÍ
Spanish painter

PLÁCIDO DOMINGO
Spanish singer

GLORIA ESTEFAN
Cuban-American singer

GABRIEL GARCÍA MÁRQUEZ
Colombian writer

FRANCISCO JOSÉ DE GOYA
Spanish painter

JULIO IGLESIAS
Spanish singer

RAUL JULIA
Puerto Rican actor

FRIDA KAHLO
Mexican painter

JOSÉ MARTÍ
Cuban revolutionary and poet

RITA MORENO
Puerto Rican singer and actress

PABLO NERUDA
Chilean poet and diplomat

OCTAVIO PAZ
Mexican poet and critic

PABLO PICASSO
Spanish artist

ANTHONY QUINN
Mexican-American actor

DIEGO RIVERA
Mexican painter

LINDA RONSTADT
Mexican-American singer

ANTONIO LÓPEZ DE SANTA ANNA
Mexican general and politician

GEORGE SANTAYANA
Spanish philosopher and poet

JUNÍPERO SERRA
Spanish missionary and explorer

LEE TREVINO
Mexican-American golfer

PANCHO VILLA
Mexican revolutionary

CHELSEA HOUSE PUBLISHERS

HISPANICS OF ACHIEVEMENT

Rodolfo Cardona

The Spanish language and many other elements of Spanish culture are present in the United States today and have been since the country's earliest beginnings. Some of these elements have come directly from the Iberian Peninsula; others have come indirectly, by way of Mexico, the Caribbean basin, and the countries of Central and South America.

Spanish culture has influenced America in many subtle ways, and consequently many Americans remain relatively unaware of the extent of its impact. The vast majority of them recognize the influence of Spanish culture in America, but they often do not realize the great importance and long history of that influence. This is partly because Americans have tended to judge the Hispanic influence in the United States in statistical terms rather than to look closely at the ways in which individual Hispanics have profoundly affected American culture. For this reason, it is fitting that Americans obtain more than a passing acquaintance with the origins of these Spanish cultural elements and gain an understanding of how they have been woven into the fabric of American society.

It is well documented that Spanish seafarers were the first to explore and colonize many of the early territories of what is today called the United States of America. For this reason, stu-

dents of geography discover Hispanic names all over the map of
the United States. For instance, the Strait of Juan de Fuca was
named after the Spanish explorer who first navigated the waters
of the Pacific Northwest; the names of states such as Arizona (arid
zone), Montana (mountain), Florida (thus named because it was
reached on Easter Sunday, which in Spanish is called the feast of
Pascua Florida), and California (named after a fictitious land in
one of the first and probably the most popular among the Spanish
novels of chivalry, *Amadis of Gaul*) are all derived from Spanish;
and there are numerous mountains, rivers, canyons, towns, and
cities with Spanish names throughout the United States.

Not only explorers but many other illustrious figures in
Spanish history have helped define American culture. For example, the 13th-century king of Spain, Alfonso X, also known as
the Learned, may be unknown to the majority of Americans, but
his work on the codification of Spanish law has greatly influenced
the evolution of American law, particularly in the jurisdictions of
the Southwest. For this contribution a statue of him stands in the
rotunda of the Capitol in Washington, D.C. Likewise, the name
Diego Rivera may be unfamiliar to most Americans, but this
Mexican painter influenced many American artists whose paintings, commissioned during the Great Depression and the New
Deal era of the 1930s, adorn the walls of government buildings
throughout the United States. In recent years the contributions of
Puerto Ricans, Mexicans, Mexican Americans (Chicanos), and
Cubans in American cities such as Boston, Chicago, Los Angeles,
Miami, Minneapolis, New York, and San Antonio have been
enormous.

The importance of the Spanish language in this vast cultural
complex cannot be overstated. Spanish, after all, is second only to
English as the most widely spoken of Western languages within
the United States as well as in the entire world. The popularity of
the Spanish language in America has a long history.

In addition to Spanish exploration of the New World, the
great Spanish literary tradition served as a vehicle for bringing the

language and culture to America. Interest in Spanish literature in America began when English immigrants brought with them translations of Spanish masterpieces of the Golden Age. As early as 1683, private libraries in Philadelphia and Boston contained copies of the first picaresque novel, *Lazarillo de Tormes*, translations of Francisco de Quevedo's *Los Sueños*, and copies of the immortal epic of reality and illusion *Don Quixote*, by the great Spanish writer Miguel de Cervantes. It would not be surprising if Cotton Mather, the arch-Puritan, read *Don Quixote* in its original Spanish, if only to enrich his vocabulary in preparation for his writing *La fe del cristiano en 24 artículos de la Institución de Cristo, enviada a los españoles para que abran sus ojos* (The Christian's Faith in 24 Articles of the Institution of Christ, Sent to the Spaniards to Open Their Eyes), published in Boston in 1699.

Over the years, Spanish authors and their works have had a vast influence on American literature—from Washington Irving, John Steinbeck, and Ernest Hemingway in the novel to Henry Wadsworth Longfellow and Archibald MacLeish in poetry. Such important American writers as James Fenimore Cooper, Edgar Allan Poe, Walt Whitman, Mark Twain, and Herman Melville all owe a sizable debt to the Spanish literary tradition. Some writers, such as Willa Cather and Maxwell Anderson, who explored Spanish themes they came into contact with in the American Southwest and Mexico, were influenced less directly but no less profoundly.

Important contributions to a knowledge of Spanish culture in the United States were also made by many lesser known individuals—teachers, publishers, historians, entrepreneurs, and others—with a love for Spanish culture. One of the most significant of these contributions was made by Abiel Smith, a Harvard College graduate of the class of 1764, when he bequeathed stock worth $20,000 to Harvard for the support of a professor of French and Spanish. By 1819 this endowment had produced enough income to appoint a professor, and the philologist and humanist George Ticknor became the first holder of the Abiel

Smith Chair, which was the very first endowed Chair at Harvard University. Other illustrious holders of the Smith Chair would include the poets Henry Wadsworth Longfellow and James Russell Lowell.

A highly respected teacher and scholar, Ticknor was also a collector of Spanish books, and as such he made a very special contribution to America's knowledge of Spanish culture. He was instrumental in amassing for Harvard libraries one of the first and most impressive collections of Spanish books in the United States. He also had a valuable personal collection of Spanish books and manuscripts, which he bequeathed to the Boston Public Library.

With the creation of the Abiel Smith Chair, Spanish language and literature courses became part of the curriculum at Harvard, which also went on to become the first American university to offer graduate studies in Romance languages. Other colleges and universities throughout the United States gradually followed Harvard's example, and today Spanish language and culture may be studied at most American institutions of higher learning.

No discussion of the Spanish influence in the United States, however brief, would be complete without a mention of the Spanish influence on art. Important American artists such as John Singer Sargent, James A. M. Whistler, Thomas Eakins, and Mary Cassatt all explored Spanish subjects and experimented with Spanish techniques. Virtually every serious American artist living today has studied the work of the Spanish masters as well as the great 20th-century Spanish painters Salvador Dalí, Joan Miró, and Pablo Picasso.

The most pervasive Spanish influence in America, however, has probably been in music. Compositions such as Leonard Bernstein's *West Side Story*, the Latinization of William Shakespeare's *Romeo and Juliet* set in New York's Puerto Rican quarter, and Aaron Copland's *Salon Mexico* are two obvious examples. In general, one can hear the influence of Latin rhythms—from tango to mambo, from guaracha to salsa—in virtually every form of American music.

This series of biographies, which Chelsea House has published under the general title HISPANICS OF ACHIEVEMENT, constitutes further recognition of—and a renewed effort to bring forth to the consciousness of America's young people—the contributions that Hispanic people have made not only in the United States but throughout the civilized world. The men and women who are featured in this series have attained a high level of accomplishment in their respective fields of endeavor and have made a permanent mark on American society.

The title of this series must be understood in its broadest possible sense: The term *Hispanics* is intended to include Spaniards, Spanish Americans, and individuals from many countries whose language and culture have either direct or indirect Spanish origins. The names of many of the people included in this series will be immediately familiar; others will be less recognizable. All, however, have attained recognition within their own countries, and often their fame has transcended their borders.

The series HISPANICS OF ACHIEVEMENT thus addresses the attainments and struggles of Hispanic people in the United States and seeks to tell the stories of individuals whose personal and professional lives in some way reflect the larger Hispanic experience. These stories are exemplary of what human beings can accomplish, often against daunting odds and by extraordinary personal sacrifice, where there is conviction and determination. Fray Junípero Serra, the 18th-century Spanish Franciscan missionary, is one such individual. Although in very poor health, he devoted the last 15 years of his life to the foundation of missions throughout California—then a mostly unsettled expanse of land—in an effort to bring a better life to Native Americans through the cultivation of crafts and animal husbandry. An example from recent times, the Mexican-American labor leader Cesar Chavez battled bitter opposition and made untold personal sacrifices in his effort to help poor agricultural workers who have been exploited for decades on farms throughout the Southwest.

The talent with which each one of these men and women may have been endowed required dedication and hard work to develop and become fully realized. Many of them have enjoyed rewards for their efforts during their own lifetime, whereas others have died poor and unrecognized. For some it took a long time to achieve their goals, for others success came at an early age, and for still others the struggle continues. All of them, however, stand out as people whose lives have made a difference, whose achievements we need to recognize today and should continue to honor in the future.

Pablo Picasso

GUERNICA

On April 12, 1931, thousands of jubilant Spaniards sang and danced in the streets, celebrating the birth of Spain's Second Republic. Never in their lifetimes had there been so much hope for the future of Spain. The Spanish monarchy, which had grown corrupt and ineffective, had been abolished, the hated dictator General Miguel Primo de Rivera had been ousted, and democracy had won the day. There truly was reason to celebrate.

But the festivities were short-lived. The Great Depression, which swept the United States and Europe during the 1930s, brought higher unemployment and more widespread hunger to an already impoverished Spain. As hard times got harder, demonstrators hit the streets of Madrid to demand change, opposing political alliances were formed, and the new Spanish government was under attack on two fronts. On one side were the wealthy classes and the Catholic church, which retained control over thousands of untilled acres of land, the schools, the mines, and the factories. On the other side were the peasants, the miners, and the factory workers. The peasants, who depended on the land for their survival, called for reform of the laws governing land distribution and use. Workers cried out for free public schools, respect-

Pablo Picasso, photographed in 1935. Already acknowledged as the most important figure in modern art, Picasso was also a passionate champion of social justice and a supporter of the democratic movement in his native Spain.

15

able wages, and safer working conditions. But their calls fell on deaf ears as those in power did whatever they could to hold on to their wealth and refused to compromise on social and political reforms. Consequently, independence movements gained momentum, and there was increasing support for and membership in anarchist groups, which advocated abolishing government completely in favor of direct rule by the people.

Spain plummeted into civil strife in the fall of 1934 as right-wing elements clashed with demonstrating peasants and workers throughout the country. In October of that year, miners organized a strike with the aim of improving working conditions in the mining region of Asturias. The government, still outwardly democratic but increasingly influenced by right-wing legislators, authorized General Francisco Franco to restore order. Franco assembled a powerful force and ordered his men to open fire on the striking miners. More than 1,000 workers were killed in the massacre, and another 30,000 were arrested and imprisoned. The country's military had actually waged war on its own citizenry. Throughout Spain, people began quietly collecting weapons and storing them in attics and cellars.

As the right-wing threat to the Republic intensified, prodemocracy factions formed a coalition party, the Popular Front, with the goal of defending and preserving the Republic. Following suit, the Monarchists and Fascists formed the National Front party. In an election held in January 1936, the Popular Front was victorious, but the right-wing elements declared the election invalid and would not give in to the people's will.

Franco emerged as the leader of the right-wing Nationalists. With the support of the country's conservative Catholics, powerful landowners, and wealthy businessmen, he felt he could seize control of Spain. Once he had the support of these most conservative elements of Spanish society, Franco formed alliances with other insurgent generals and launched a military campaign to topple the Republican government. On November 7, 1936, the Nationalists advanced on the city of Madrid. The fighting continued for days, but the people of the city would not surrender. Some 15,000 of them had dug trenches along the city limits and were steadfast in their effort to beat back the Fascist aggressors. To the surprise of the Nationalists, the Republican Loyalists were totally committed to defending their government and declared their willingness to die in the name of freedom and democracy. Spain was plunged into civil war.

Spanish Fascist leader Francisco Franco (center) and German chancellor Adolf Hitler (left), photographed during a 1940 meeting. When Franco's forces rose up against the Spanish Republic in 1936, Hitler's Nazi regime quickly came to his aid with troops and modern weaponry.

The shelling of Madrid continued, but Franco focused his attention on the north, and in particular on Guernica, the ancient capital of the Basque Republic. He believed that if he could seize control of the Basque Provinces, where the vast majority of the people were Republican Loyalists, he would deal the Republican cause a possibly fatal blow. Franco asked Germany's Fascist dictator, Adolf Hitler, on whose support he greatly relied, to send warplanes to bomb Guernica.

During the 1930s, fascism was on the rise throughout Europe. Not only was Franco consolidating power in Spain; Hitler, the leader of Germany's Nazi party, had become German chancellor in 1933 and had already formed an alliance with the Italian Fascist Benito Mussolini. Their plan was nothing less than world domination, and by the late 1930s they had already equipped themselves militarily for a campaign to achieve that end. Dropping bombs on the civilian population of Guernica would be an easy mission for the German bombers; it would provide an opportunity to study the effects of different kinds of bombs; and, most important, it would advance the cause of fascism.

Most of the citizens of Guernica were shopping in the town square during the afternoon of April 26, 1937, when the roar of 43 German warplanes shattered the busy, happy chatter of the marketplace. Fear and then panic struck the hearts of the townspeople as the bombers flew low overhead. Children screamed, and men and women ran for cover, some seeking safety within the walls of their homes. But the German bombs rained down on Guernica, and within minutes the town square was soaked with blood. When the bombing finally stopped, a relative quiet fell over the village that just three hours before had been a bustling scene of people happily going about their daily routines. In a flash, the town had been devastated.

German warplanes rain death upon the Basque city of Guernica on April 26, 1937. Aiming to demoralize the Republican cause and test their bombing techniques, the Fascists killed 1,600 civilians, injured 1,000 more, and destroyed 70 percent of Guernica's buildings.

Now the twisted and torn bodies of the dead littered the bloodstained streets. Homes and shops were blasted and burned, reduced to smoldering ruins, and the cries of the maimed and wounded could be heard faintly above the rubble.

During the next four days, detailed accounts of the bombing of Guernica were published in newspapers around the world. Franco tried to blame the town's destruction on Communist factions, but witnesses to the attack quickly exposed this as a lie. After the Guernica raid, Franco became an international pariah, and the Fascist cause was widely condemned. Still, Franco had his supporters—among them Hitler, Mus-

solini, wealthy Spaniards, and the Roman Catholic church—and powerful democracies such as Great Britain and the United States took Franco's side indirectly by refusing to aid the poorly equipped Republicans.

In his studio at 7, rue des Grands-Augustins, in Paris, France, the great Spanish painter and sculptor Pablo Picasso, known throughout the world as an artistic visionary of revolutionary proportions, was shocked as he read the detailed accounts of the senseless bloodshed at Guernica in the French newspapers *Le Soir* and *L'Humanité*. The photos taken in the days following the raid were horrifying. Some 1,600 innocent people had been slaughtered and 1,000 more

To express his outrage over the destruction of the Basque capital, Picasso painted his mural Guernica *in 1937. A heartfelt condemnation of war as well as a modern masterpiece,* Guernica *is now housed in a special annex of Spain's great Prado Museum.*

wounded in a matter of a few hours, and about 70 percent of Guernica was destroyed. Picasso was moved to tears of rage.

Great artist that he was, he was also moved by a powerful urge to create. Picasso had been searching for a theme for a mural he had been commissioned to paint for the Spanish Pavilion at the Paris World's Fair. The Guernica bombing had affected him so deeply that he turned to his work with a burst of creative energy. He had found his theme, and with characteristic urgency he set about depicting the unspeakable horror of fascism in one of the century's most disturbing masterpieces.

ELEGANT GYPSY

Pablo Ruiz Picasso was born on October 25, 1881, in Málaga, Spain, to José Ruiz Blasco and María Picasso López. (At the age of 21, he began to use his mother's name exclusively, both as a tribute to her and because the name was more unusual). As one account has it, there were complications with the birth, and the family members who had gathered that day for the occasion were severely disappointed when the midwife regretfully informed them that the baby boy was stillborn. But José's brother Salvador, who was a medical doctor, was not so sure the midwife was correct. He leaned over the motionless infant, exhaled a puff of cigar smoke into the baby's tiny nostrils, and suddenly, to the excitement and delight of all present, he who would eventually become one of the greatest artists of the 20th century let out a cry and joined the world of the living.

Tall and thin with blue eyes, pale skin, and a blond beard, José Ruiz Blasco had an appearance that was uncommon in southern Spain. Because of his light coloring he was nicknamed "the Englishman." He had a wonderful sense of humor and liked to socialize in the town's cafés, especially the Café de Chinitas,

Pablo Picasso, at the age of four, photographed with his sister Lola. The son of a well-known painter, young Pablo was already making amazingly detailed drawings of plants and animals when this photo was taken. "I never did any childish drawings," he later stated proudly.

where he would spend hours chatting with local artists about his greatest love, painting. Ruiz was well known in Málaga for his skill as a painter, particularly of nature scenes.

María Picasso, a petite, dark-haired, dark-eyed woman, was 17 years younger than Ruiz. Their meeting was arranged by their respective families. Before they could marry, however, Ruiz had to find suitable employment. Although Spain has produced many great painters and has one of the finest art museums in the world, the Prado, painters generally did not enjoy very high social status there, and they were certainly not considered good prospects for marriage. In July 1879, Ruiz took a position as assistant teacher of drawing at the San Telmo School of Arts and Crafts, and in June of the following year, thanks to his brother Salvador's influence, he was named curator of Málaga's Municipal Museum. Finally, on December 8, 1880, José and María were married at the Church of Santiago. She became pregnant almost immediately thereafter.

As a child, Pablo was pampered by women; not only his mother but his grandmother, two aunts, and a maid lived in the house and tended constantly to his needs and wishes. Pablo was in good hands, but José Ruiz found it increasingly difficult to provide for this extended family. The situation worsened when the Municipal Museum did away with his curator's post. In order to reduce expenses, the family moved into smaller quarters, an apartment where the landlord agreed to accept paintings as rent.

In December 1884, a devastating earthquake hit Málaga, and the family was forced to move again, this time into a house owned by José's friend and fellow painter Antonio Muñoz Degrain, who was living in Rome. This unsettling time made a lasting impression on the young Pablo, who watched his father and mother, who was pregnant with her second child, hastily packing as the earth trembled. María gave birth to a daughter, Lola, on December 28.

The Spain of Picasso's youth was in rapid decline. For centuries, Spanish explorers had sailed to distant, exotic shores in search of riches and the most direct sea trade routes. In the course of their journeys, these seafarers frequently invaded and enslaved native populations and claimed lands for the Spanish crown. With holdings in North Africa, the Caribbean, Guam, and the Philippines acquired in this way, Spain was able to exploit the people and resources of these colonies and to build a large and powerful empire. But during the 19th century, Spain slowly began to lose its footing as a colonial power as independence movements in Mexico and South America pushed the Spaniards out. Also, from 1868 to 1878, and again during the 1890s, rebels waged war on the Spanish colonial government on the Caribbean island of Cuba. With the empire crumbling, Spain fell on hard economic times, and dissent became as loud and widespread at home as it had been in the colonies.

Amid this chaos, the young Picasso was showing early signs of artistic genius. At the age of four he was making impressive drawings of flowers and animals to the delight of his cousins, who sat in amazement as they watched a donkey or rooster, rendered in detail and with great accuracy, take form under the little boy's pencil. The sketches were remarkably advanced. Later, Picasso recalled, "I never did any childish drawings. Never. Not even when I was a very small boy." He also used scissors to cut shapes from paper and used light to project their shadows on the wall. His father watched with pride as his son made drawing after drawing, and Pablo worshiped his father, who although not a great artist, was not without considerable talent. The two were inseparable—until the boy began to attend school and had to let go of his father's hand each day when they said good-bye.

In 1895, the 14-year-old Picasso painted this portrait of his mother, María. María Picasso, who doted on her firstborn son, was concerned when Pablo showed little aptitude for traditional school-work; by the time he was a teenager, however, she realized that he was destined to be an artist.

From the start, Pablo was bored in class and spent most of his time watching the clock, gazing out the window, and daydreaming. What little effort he did make at reading and arithmetic almost never yielded encouraging results, so it was not surprising when he eventually lost interest completely. He usually turned from his studies to sketch the teacher, his classmates, or some object in the room. His parents worried about him; they knew he was not stupid and that he had, at least for a while, tried to apply himself, but they saw too that his progress was dismal. Dyslexia or some other learning disorder may have been responsible for Pablo's problems at school, but at that time learning disorders had not yet been identified by psychologists and educators.

María gave birth to a second daughter, Concepción, also called Conchita, on October 30, 1887, and José, who had been struggling to support his family by painting and teaching privately, found himself under even greater financial pressure. Consequently, when in 1891 he was offered a job teaching drawing at the newly opened Da Guarda Institute in La Coruña, a bustling port city in the northwest corner of Spain, he decided he had to take it, even though it meant that he and his family would have to leave their beloved Málaga. In October, José, María, and their three children boarded a ship bound for La Coruña, leaving behind the other family members.

The following year, José decided that it was time for his son to begin formal art training and enrolled Pablo at the school where he taught. There the boy suddenly showed an aptitude that was in shocking contrast with his previous attempts at learning to read and write. He now learned quickly and received excellent grades on his examinations, impressing both his teachers and his classmates. Eventually, one classmate in particular, a girl named Angeles Mendez Gil, attracted his attention. But the girl's disapproving middle-class family, wanting to discourage any union between their daughter and the son of a poor painter, transferred her to a school in Pamplona. Pablo had begun collecting his drawings in albums; now the heartbroken youth made references to his lost love in their pages.

The pain that the smitten 13-year-old Pablo felt when Angeles left for Pamplona was small compared to the deep sorrow, resentment, and guilt he experienced in 1895 as he watched his sister Conchita die of diphtheria. José and María had done all they could to nurse the girl back to health. Doctors came and went with few words of encouragement. The situation was hopeless, but Pablo thought that he could save his sister by making a pact with God. He offered to sacrifice his artistic talent for his sister's sake, promising never to paint again if only her life could be spared. Then, struck with the realization that he had made a promise he would never want to keep, he began secretly hoping that Conchita would die so that he would not have to keep his word and give up his art. Then, when Conchita drew her last breath, Pablo was devastated by guilt, believing that by bargaining with God he had somehow brought about his sister's death.

Having left friends and loved ones behind in Málaga, José Ruiz had been unhappy since moving to La Coruña. Now the tragic loss of his youngest daughter plunged him into a deep depression. He swore never to paint again, handing his brushes and paints to Pablo, who was deeply moved by his father's profound sense of loss. It was clear to both father and son that a change of scene was needed to help the family get a fresh start.

José applied for and received a transfer to Barcelona. Before leaving, however, he arranged for a show of his son's paintings in the back room of a small knickknack shop. Then the family boarded a train for Málaga, where they would spend the summer before settling in Barcelona. On the way they stopped in Madrid, Spain's capital, where they visited the Prado. There the young Picasso gazed at masterpieces by Goya, Velázquez, and other great masters. Once in Málaga, the family stayed with Pablo's uncle Salvador, who was so impressed with his nephew's work that he set him up with a studio and a small allowance. He made Pablo promise to go to Mass regularly and receive Communion. Salvador stressed the importance of regular church attendance by telling Pablo that if the boy failed to attend he would not take him to the bullfights. Picasso later recalled that this was very effective, as he "would have gone to Communion 20 times for a chance of going to the bullfights."

A drawing class at the Llotja, Barcelona's school of fine arts, at the beginning of the 20th century. Picasso entered the prestigious school in 1895; though only 14, he was so advanced that he breezed through his classes and had ample time to explore Barcelona's café society.

When young Picasso arrived in Barcelona with his parents and sister in the fall of 1895, the city was in turmoil. The dissolution of the Spanish Empire, the resultant economic depression, the unraveling of the hopes and dreams of the Spanish people, and the revolt of both intellectuals and the working classes combined to create a swell of social and political awareness throughout Spain and particularly in Barcelona. During this unsettling yet exciting time, Picasso enrolled at the Llotja, the city's prestigious school of fine arts.

But for Picasso, the Llotja provided little in terms of real learning. In fact, the young genius met the class requirements so easily that he had ample time to roam the streets of Barcelona with his friend and fellow artist Manuel Pallarès. Together they wandered from café to café, their favorite being the infamous Eden Concert, which the more righteous people of Bar-

Picasso made this charcoal drawing, Study of a Torso, After a Plaster Cast, *at the age of 14. Having achieved a mastery of realistic detail that made him the equal of any adult painter, the teenager was already determined to revolutionize the art world.*

celona believed was frequented only by those beyond any hope of salvation. At the Eden, Picasso and Pallarès met the brothers Angel and Mateu de Soto, Joaquim Bas, and Ramon Reventós, with whom they visited the city's Chinatown district and its notorious red-light district.

Picasso was fascinated by the city's dark underside, but he was never consumed by it; he continued to work with extraordinary skill and passion. During his early days in Barcelona, he produced a number of works on the theme of religious struggle. Several of these—*Christ Blessing the Devil, Altar to the Blessed Virgin, First Communion,* and *The Holy Family in Egypt*—revealed his personal agony over the forces of good and evil in his own life and thus a remarkable maturity for a young teenager. He also won awards for his work very early on. When he was 15 years old, *Science and Charity* brought him an honorable mention at the Madrid General Fine Arts Exhibition of 1897 and a gold medal at the Málaga Provincial Exhibition that same year.

Picasso enjoyed the limelight, but he was not as interested in painting canvases that would please people as he was in breaking with traditions and establishing himself as an innovator. Acceptance had come to him quite easily; even painters of his father's generation by now recognized him as their equal if

A view of Horta de Ebro, the isolated Spanish village where Picasso spent several weeks in 1898. Exhilarated by the beauty of Horta and the freedom of outdoor life, Picasso returned to Barcelona with the vision and energy he needed to become a world-class painter.

not their superior. But Picasso's ambition was without limit; although only in his teens, he already dreamed of revolutionizing painting. He knew that if he was serious about his art—and he was—he had to go to Madrid to undergo the most demanding artistic training his country had to offer.

In the fall of 1897, Picasso enrolled in Madrid's Royal Academy of San Fernando, his expenses paid through a concerted effort by his parents, aunts, and uncle. To his dismay, he soon found that even at San Fernando he was barely challenged, and so he spent little time there. Once more he roamed the city streets, frequenting the cafés, filling his sketchbook with pencil drawings of nocturnal bohemians.

But this time the café life caught up with the young artist, and he became ill. *Picasso Bewildered,* a self-portrait he drew during that time, reflects the sad physical state to which he had driven himself. Once he recovered, he returned to Barcelona, where he was reunited with his friend Pallarès. Seeing that Picasso needed some time away from the city, Pallarès suggested that they visit his parents in Horta de Ebro, a tiny, isolated mountain village where they made their home.

The weeks Picasso spent in Horta brought about a powerful transformation of his emotional life. After several days in the Pallarès house, Picasso and Pallarès, with the help of a Gypsy boy who knew the region well, explored the wild forests and mountains surrounding Horta. They slept in a cave or under the stars and huddled around a fire in the evenings to keep warm. Every few days, Pallarès's younger brother rode a mule eight miles to bring supplies to their outpost in the wilds. But the sojourn was more than a camping trip for the impressionable Picasso.

During the time they spent together in the mountains, Picasso and the Gypsy boy, who was two years younger than his artist friend, developed a deeply intimate relationship. The Gypsy boy's free, natural spirit had an irresistible attraction for Picasso. He was moved by his new acquaintance's wild, uninhibited ways, and he wanted to learn what the boy could teach him about the mysterious workings of nature. The Gypsy was also a painter, and he and Picasso spent a good part of each day sketching and painting the lush landscape around them and exchanging ideas about art. They would sometimes rise early to watch the sunrise, and after a long day of strenuous climbing along mountain ridges they would occasionally sit on a hillside in silence until nightfall and then gaze at the stars and breathe the cool mountain air.

One day, in a moment of overwhelming joy and abandon, Picasso and the Gypsy boy each cut a wrist and then pressed their wounds together, allowing their blood to intermix. As their blood mingled and ran down their forearms, dripping onto the ground and seeping into the earth, the boys vowed their loyalty to each other forever. But despite their having bonded through this ancient ritual, deep down they both knew that their union was ultimately impossible, that their encounter, however meaningful, would of necessity be brief. Early one morning, Picasso rose from his bed of grass to find that the Gypsy boy had disappeared silently during the night. Rather than bear the incredible weight of their impossible love, the Gypsy had left his artist friend and returned to the forests alone.

In February 1899, Picasso returned alone to Barcelona. His journey into the idyllic world of Horta, an indescribable mystical journey, had transformed him. Now he was attuned to the Gypsy in his soul, the inspiration that would propel him to greatness.

CHANGING HUES

Picasso at the age of 23, photographed in Paris. During his early twenties, the young artist divided his time between Paris and Barcelona; though he had his first successful exhibit in Barcelona, he ultimately decided to settle permanently in the French capital.

On December 10, 1898, after a series of humiliating military defeats in the Spanish-American War, Spain was forced to sign the Treaty of Paris, agreeing to withdraw from Cuba and ceding Puerto Rico, Guam, and the Philippines to the United States. For Spaniards, the shock was almost unbearable. They called the events culminating in the signing of the treaty *el desastre* (the disaster): not only was the defeat humiliating, but without the great material resources of its former colonies Spain had little on which to build its future. Only the northern African colony of Morocco, located across the Strait of Gibraltar, remained in Spain's possession; but there, too, the spirit of rebellion was moving among the people.

Spain fell into a state of dire economic hardship and social despair. Workers lost their jobs, and some 3 million peasants, unable to claw a living from the land in such hard times, wandered about the countryside in a desperate search for work. About a quarter million Spaniards had died in battle or of yellow fever in a losing cause in Cuba and Puerto Rico, and now the wounded survivors and their families struggled to put their lives back together. The industrialists who had grown wealthy on the labors of Cubans, Puerto Ricans, and Filipinos had less to worry about, but the vast

majority of Spaniards now had little on which to base
their hopes.

Out of such hardship often comes desperation,
and out of desperation sometimes comes revolution.
At the end of the 19th century in Spain, intellectuals
launched an attack on the country's ruling institutions—the monarchy, the Catholic church, and the
military—and decried the country's history of coloni-
alism and exploitation. Inspired by the revolutionary
activity then taking place in Russia, Spanish workers
and peasants joined in the call for change, demonstrating in the streets for land reform, better pay, and
improved working conditions. Leftist political ideas
took hold, particularly in the northern region of
Catalonia, where the radical Spanish anarchist and
separatist movements were born.

But the restlessness that characterized Spain at that
time was not one stirred by hope. By the time Picasso
arrived in Barcelona in February 1899, Spain was in a
state of national depression. This depression is reflected in Picasso's work during this period. *The Kiss
of Death, The Cry of Death, Two Agonies,* and *Priest
Visiting a Dying Man* are just a few of the pieces he
painted during this period that reflect the malaise that
had fallen over Spain. These and other paintings from
this period also reveal Picasso's own personal despair
and preoccupation with death.

Soon after arriving in Barcelona, Picasso decided
not to return to the Llotja and took a room at a
hellishly filthy brothel. It is difficult to guess why he
chose to live amid such squalor, but Picasso's fascination with the underside of society and his insatiable
hunger for intense experiences might partly explain
the decision. In any event, he continued to work,
sharing a studio with another artist, Carles Casagemas,
whom he had recently met. The two men became
very close friends.

Picasso began to frequent a cabaret called Els Quatre Gats (The Four Cats), a lively hive of intellectual conversation where painters and writers conspired to carve out a new century in art, literature, and philosophy. Some of the personalities that graced the place were Pompeu Gener and Jaume Brossa, two scholars who introduced Picasso to the writings and ideas of the German philosopher Friedrich Nietzsche; the painters Santiago Rusiñol and Ramon Casas; and Picasso's friend Pallarès. Els Quatre Gats was also a place where artists exhibited their work, and Picasso showed some of his drawings there, mostly portraits, in February 1900.

The owner of Els Quatre Gats subscribed to a number of French art magazines, and Picasso pored over them for hours each day. Soon he wanted more than anything to go to Paris, to gain exposure to French art and to immerse himself in the creative life of that great city. When Picasso told his father about his desire to go to Paris, the elder artist understood and purchased a round-trip train ticket for his son. Picasso was thrilled. Not only was he leaving Spain for the first time in his life, but he was going to Paris, then considered the art capital of the world. He invited Pallarès and Casagemas to join him, but only Casagemas was able to. As the two young painters climbed aboard their train, Picasso's parents waved good-bye to their son from the station platform.

When he arrived in Paris, it was as if Picasso had been released from a cave into a bright new world. He lived nowhere in particular—spending most of his waking hours on the streets, in the cafés, or in the city's museums and sleeping in various studios and cheap hotels. He also went to the theater, although he often had difficulty following the action, the dialogue being, of course, in French. He exposed himself to French art, and his work from this time was most clearly

Picasso at work in his studio on the boulevard de Clichy in 1901, watched by a group of friends who include the art dealer Pere Mañach (right). Due to Mañach's willingness to subsidize his work, the once-impoverished Picasso was able to pay his rent and live comfortably while he developed his art.

influenced by the painters Pierre-Auguste Renoir and Henri de Toulouse-Lautrec. Although he did come to know a number of young French women and had a few girlfriends during his early days in Paris, Picasso at first felt very much a stranger in Paris and associated mostly with fellow Spaniards.

One of the Spaniards Picasso got to know in Paris was a Catalan factory owner and art dealer named Pere Mañach. So impressed was Mañach by the young painter's work that he offered Picasso 150 francs a month for whatever paintings he completed. As one could eat for about two francs a day, Mañach's offer was substantial enough that it would enable Picasso to rent a small studio and live relatively comfortably.

Picasso accepted the offer, but he would not stay in Paris; he decided to go back to Spain.

Picasso returned to Barcelona, tired of it quickly, and settled in Madrid for the winter. Mañach continued to send money each month to Picasso's garret. In February 1901, Picasso received the tragic news that his friend Casagemas had shot and killed himself.

Deeply saddened by his friend's suicide, Picasso returned to Barcelona and immersed himself in his work. Then he received a letter from Mañach informing him that the well-respected Parisian art dealer Ambroise Vollard was prepared to exhibit his work. Picasso returned to Paris, this time with his friend Jaume Andreu Bonsons, and in May 1901 moved into Casagemas's old studio at 130, boulevard de Clichy,

Le Moulin de la Galette, *painted by Picasso in 1901. Parisian nightlife had fascinated many French painters of the 19th century, and Picasso followed such masters as Renoir and Toulouse-Lautrec in depicting the cafés and dance halls of the dazzling metropolis.*

which he shared with Mañach, who had also taken up residence there.

A fascination with Parisian nightlife— of which *The Absinthe Drinker, Picasso in a Top Hat, French Cancan,* and *At the Moulin Rouge,* all from 1901, are perhaps the best-known examples—continued to be evident in Picasso's work. The influence of Toulouse-Lautrec, who throughout his life had a fascination for Parisian cafés and cabarets, was especially apparent in Picasso's work during this period.

By most accounts, the exhibit was a success, being favorably reviewed in a number of art publications and causing the Parisian art lovers to sit up and take notice of the new talent in their midst. Fifteen works were sold even before the exhibit opened, and a particularly complimentary review was written by the critic Félicien Fagus in *Revue Blanche,* an important art journal. The exhibit also occasioned a meeting between Picasso and the poet and art critic Max Jacob, who would become one of the artist's most devout admirers and closest friends.

But Picasso continued to be troubled by Casagemas's suicide, and much of his work during this period reflected his somber mood. In the summer of 1901, he painted *Portrait of the Dead Casagemas, The Death of Casagemas,* and *Evocation (The Burial of Casagemas),* the three works most obviously related to his friend's death. (The last of these recalled *Burial of Count Orgaz* by the great 17th-century Spanish artist El Greco.)

Picasso's work during this time increasingly revealed a general preoccupation with human suffering and death. Most notably, during the period from 1901 to about 1904, referred to as his blue period, Picasso abandoned the vibrant color of his earlier work and instead painted mostly in shades of blue. His subjects were the sick, the hungry, the poor, the lonely, and the crippled. Among the best-known works from the so-called Paris blue period are *Child Holding a Dove, Harlequin, Two Saltimbanques,* and *Self-Portrait.*

After receiving some money from his father, Picasso returned to Barcelona and was reunited with his family in early 1902. There he shared a studio with another artist and resumed his work in blue and blue-green hues. Picasso was fixated on the miseries of poverty, psychological depression, and human struggle. For example, in 1902 he painted *The Two Sisters, Woman with a Scarf,* and *Two Women at a Bar,* all dealing with the themes of solitude and loneliness and done in the same sad bluish palette.

In October of that year, Picasso once again returned to Paris, this time with his friend Josep Rocarol, who was also a painter. Before leaving, however, the young men each paid the necessary fee to avoid military service. When they arrived in Paris, they rented a room in the Montparnasse section of the city, but soon Picasso was on his own again, checking in and out of one cheap hotel after another. While Picasso was staying at the Hôtel du Maroc, he was visited by Max Jacob, who invited the artist to move in with him. Picasso accepted the invitation and settled into a routine of drawing and painting by night and sleeping by day.

What Jacob had referred to as "poverty coupled with genius" was driving Picasso further into despair, and the artist, fully aware of his extraordinary talent, was now anxious to achieve greater recognition. He had had high hopes for an exhibit of his work that was presented by Berthe Weill, but none of his paintings were sold there. While the exhibit was still on, the critic Charles Morice wrote the following in the *Mercure de France:*

> It is extraordinary, this sterile sadness which weighs down the entire work of this very young man.... He seems a young god trying to remake

the world. But a dark god. Most of the faces he paints grimace; not a smile. His world is no more habitable than lepers' houses. And his painting itself is sick. Incurably? I do not know. But certainly there is a strength there, a gift, a talent. . . . Is this frighteningly precocious child not fated to bestow the consecration of a masterpiece on the negative sense of living, the illness from which he more than anyone else seems to be suffering?

Another man who described Picasso's work in print was the poet Guillaume Apollinaire. Of the blue period, he wrote the following:

These children, who have no one to caress them, understand everything. These women, whom no one loves now, are remembering. They shrink back into the shadows as if into some ancient church. They disappear at daybreak, having attained consolation through silence. Old men stand about, wrapped in icy fog. These old men have the right to beg without humility.

In January 1903, Picasso returned once again to Barcelona, and what Morice referred to as the "stark sadness" of Picasso's work intensified. During the next year he produced some 50 sketches and paintings, including a portrait of the one-eyed *Celestina, The Old Guitarist,* and *The Blindman's Meal,* all strong examples of Picasso's obsession with human misery and despair in the monochromatic blue-green hue. With these and other paintings from the blue period, Picasso seems to ask why there is so much suffering in the world and why, if there is a God, does he allow his children to know so much pain and misery.

In the spring of the following year, accompanied by his friend the painter Sebastián Junyent, Picasso returned to Paris, this time with clear intentions of staying in France indefinitely. He moved into a dingy studio at 13, rue Ravignan, which Max Jacob called Le Bateau Lavoir (the laundry boat) because the

Picasso met Fernande Olivier in the summer of 1904, and a year later she moved into his studio. Picasso and Olivier were to live together for seven years; her intimate memoir Picasso and His Friends, *published in 1933, is the main source of information about Picasso's early years in Paris.*

building resembled the houseboats on the Seine River on which Parisian women did their washing. One entered the building from the top floor and descended a stairway to gain access to the two dozen studios it housed. Picasso's studio was cluttered, filthy, and noisy, but a constant stream of admirers nonetheless made their way up the steep hill in Montmartre and down the stairs of Le Bateau Lavoir to spend even a brief moment with the artist.

At Le Bateau Lavoir, Picasso continued to paint his melancholy blue canvases. Examples from this period include *Woman with Helmet of Hair,* which he completed during the summer of 1904. But by this time a rose color started to creep into Picasso's paintings, suggesting a movement away from the attitude of despair that characterizes the blue period. For example, *Woman Ironing* and *Woman with a Crow,* considered among the last of the "blue" paintings, are placed in that period more because of their subject matter than because of their overall hue. They both evoke the same sadness of the earlier works of the blue period, but they have a somewhat warm, rosy glow. It has been suggested that a chance meeting with a woman played a role in this transformation in Picasso's work.

On August 4, Picasso was walking near his studio when the sky abruptly opened and a hard rain pounded the steaming pavement. He picked up a stray kitten and sheltered it from the storm, and then he suddenly found himself face-to-face with a young woman in a white linen blouse who was soaked to the skin. He handed her the kitten, and they ran off to his studio.

The young woman's name was Fernande Olivier. She was the same age as Picasso and also an artist of sorts. Picasso had already had countless girlfriends in his life, but none of those encounters had been endowed with the intimacy of his relationship with Olivier. She moved in with him in the fall.

Rose-colored circus performers and harlequins now replaced the sad, blue denizens of Picasso's world. His subjects were still people who lived on the fringe of society in relative poverty and who knew some degree of suffering, but now there was a subtle affirmation in his paintings. In early 1905, Picasso exhibited some of his circus paintings at the Galeries Serrurier, and the critic Morice described the new work in the exhibition's catalog:

There is no longer a taste for the sad, for the ugly in themselves; this premature depression, which logically must have led to the darkness of a deathly despair, is succeeded by a beneficent anomaly, a ray of light: it is the dawn of pity that comes—it is hope.

Apollinaire, too, was impressed with the work of the rose period. He wrote, "One feels that his slender acrobats, glowing in their rags, are true sons of the people: versatile, cunning, dexterous, poverty-stricken and lying." He reviewed the Serrurier exhibit in two publications, *La Revue immoraliste* and *La Plume*.

Picasso's rose period is well represented by *Two Acrobats with a Dog*, *The Harlequin's Family*, *The Acrobat's Family with a Monkey*, and *The Family of Saltimbanques*, all from 1905. That year he also produced a

After a period of depression, during which he painted in somber tones of blue, Picasso entered his so-called rose period in 1904. Though his subjects were still circus performers and others on the fringes of society, as in The Family of Saltimbanques *(1905), the rose-colored hues of the canvases reflected a note of optimism.*

sculpture, *The Jester,* and two nudes, *Dutch Girl* and *Female Nude with Bonnet,* which he painted while visiting Holland that summer.

Toward the end of 1905, Picasso made the acquaintance of Gertrude Stein and her brother Leo. She was an American, born in 1874 in Baltimore, Maryland, which she left when she was 29. She had earned a medical degree, but being independently wealthy, she had decided not to practice medicine but to move to Paris and pursue her interests in writing and art. Leo Stein was a painter and lived in Florence, Italy, for a time before joining his sister in Paris. They were an odd-looking, eccentric pair, deeply interested in art and literature. When he met the Steins at an art gallery owned by the art dealer Clovis Sagot, Picasso immediately wanted to paint Gertrude.

Picasso and Olivier became frequent visitors at the Stein home at 27, rue de Fleurus. During one visit in 1906 they met the painter Henri Matisse. One of the 20th century's great artists, Matisse loved to talk about painting, and he and Picasso often did so for hours. Apart from painting, the two artists had little in common, but the Steins often brought together artists of contrasting tastes, talents, and temperaments.

Picasso began work on a portrait of Gertrude Stein, but after some 80 or 90 sittings, he was still dissatisfied with it. In May he painted over the head and then took off for Spain with Olivier. In Barcelona, he introduced her to his family, and then they spent some time in the Pyrenees.

In 1906, Picasso produced a series of works on the theme of the coiffure. These included *La Toilette, Woman with a Comb, La Coiffure,* and *Woman Combing Her Hair,* all painted that summer and fall. Many of his paintings from that time were populated by nude boys and horses as well, which he depicted with fine lines and light earth tones.

By the time he returned to Paris toward the end of 1906 he had found a solution to the Stein portrait. After considerable struggle, he completed the portrait in a single session, depicting Stein's face as a kind of African tribal mask. The Stein portrait was to a degree the result of Picasso's interest in African art, brought about by Matisse, who had showed him some African sculpture. Matisse had thus opened a new world to Picasso, who was characteristically determined to explore it. The rose period was definitely over, and Picasso was about to start a revolution in painting and sculpture that would chart the course of 20th-century art.

C H A P T E R
F O U R

INTERSECTING PLANES

Picasso in his studio, photographed in 1909. By this point in his career, the 28-year-old artist had already fulfilled his ambition of revolutionizing the art world, first with Les Demoiselles d'Avignon *(1907) and then with his pioneering work in the development of cubism.*

It is not known exactly when Picasso began to work on what was to be the most revolutionary painting of the 20th century, *Les Demoiselles d'Avignon*, but he apparently worked on it for some time because a number of preliminary studies for the painting exist. By 1907 he felt it was complete enough to show to some of his friends. All of them—even the most sophisticated of the avant-garde—were shocked by what they saw. Leo Stein jibed: "You've been trying to paint the fourth dimension. How amusing!" Matisse thought Picasso had deliberately set out to mock the modern movement in painting. Today *Demoiselles* is recognized as the most important painting in the history of modern art, and it has been credited with liberating painting from all the conventions of the Renaissance, making possible a new vision of the world.

What is it that made this painting both so revolutionary and so disturbing? To begin with, Picasso shattered every convention of Western painting. He smashed the human form into pieces and reassembled those pieces in a startling manner that amounted to no less than an assault on all order and expectation.

Demoiselles dispensed with the traditional rules of perspective and composition, breaking with one of the most basic and traditional concerns of Western art—to make a flat surface appear to have three dimensions. Picasso emphasized that a canvas has only two dimensions. Whereas in earlier paintings scenes were composed so as to direct the viewer's glance from one part of a painting to another, *Demoiselles* does not attempt to help the viewer by any such means. Although it is difficult today to see *Demoiselles* as shocking in light of all the abstract art and bold experimentation that has followed it, the abstract art now considered typical of the 20th century would probably not exist at all if not for the bold break with tradition that Picasso made with Les Demoiselles d'Avignon.

Picasso met the French artist Georges Braque in the fall of 1907, not long after he had finished painting *Demoiselles*. When he saw the painting, Braque was thunderstruck. Upon viewing the work, he immediately recognized the genius of Picasso, who with a single canvas seemed to chart the course for all future painting. "It made me feel," Braque said, "as if someone was drinking gasoline and spitting fire."

Schooled at the École des Beaux-Arts and the Académie Humbert, Braque, like Picasso, had become aware of his talents and received substantial recognition at a young age. He was also striking in his appearance—six feet tall, handsome, and athletic—and could play entire Beethoven symphonies on the accordion. When Picasso and Braque met, there was an instant chemistry between them. Together they frequented the cafés, constantly discussing painting and the direction they thought it should take. Like two scientists obsessed with putting their theories into practice, the artists experimented individually and then met to compare the results of their efforts. So intent were they on maintaining the purity of their

The French artist Georges Braque (1882–1963) met Picasso in 1907. After seeing Demoiselles, *Braque was convinced of Picasso's genius; the two men also hit it off personally and soon joined forces to perfect the ground-breaking style known as cubism.*

experiments that they began signing their canvases on the back only, to ensure that the artist's personality or reputation did not distract the viewer from the direct experience of the work. Out of these experiments, the artistic movement called cubism was born.

The term *cubist* was first used by the critic Léon Vauxcelles to describe some of Braque's work, but eventually cubism influenced the work of sculptors and even musicians and poets. Cubism was a complex movement that had many influences, but generally it was a logical result of the postimpressionist and symbolist reaction to the formless work of the impressionists. (The symbolists had searched for images that expressed the irrational and emotional side of human experience; their theories influenced many 20th-century artists, from Paul Gauguin to Henri Matisse.) Cubists placed a strong emphasis on the abstraction of objects into their form, unlike the impressionists, who were more concerned with essences and ideas than with physical shapes and textures. Braque and the French painter Paul Cézanne had begun this shift in emphasis toward form, but Picasso's *Demoiselles* is considered by many art historians to be the most significant early step in the evolution of cubism.

Cubism sought a new resolution to the eternal problem of how to represent three dimensions on a two-dimensional canvas. Cézanne had sought to uncover the basic geometrical shapes of the cone, the sphere, and the cylinder in the objects that filled his landscapes and still lifes. Braque and Picasso, following the breakthrough of *Demoiselles,* now sliced nature into paper-thin planes and spread these planes out on their canvases.

Over the years Picasso and Braque would take cubism through an evolution of its own. The earliest phase of their experimentation is called analytic cubism because the subject is reduced to pure geometric forms and planes. Arrayed on the canvas, these parts could each be examined from several angles and under different conditions of light.

It was on a trip to Spain made with Fernande Olivier during the summer of 1909 that Picasso made many of the breakthroughs in cubism. Some art historians have theorized that the Spanish landscape itself helped inspire Picasso's innovations, for Spain's stucco houses on tiered hills tended to form geometric complexes. But just as Picasso was shaking up the artistic firmament in France, when he and Fernande reached Barcelona they found that other bold spirits in Spain had recently issued a call for radical changes in the social and political spheres. These appeals for reform in Spain had reverberated throughout the country, but the Spanish government had reacted to the fledgling reform movements with a campaign of terror. Hundreds of trade unionists were arrested. Some were tortured and even executed. The press was censored. For a time the Spanish people were subdued, but deep down their resolve to bring about political and social change was undaunted.

With the unrest at home temporarily under control, the Spanish government turned its attention to Morocco. France had already gained control of a large portion of the Spanish colony and was now threatening to take it all. Moreover, Moorish freedom fighters were resisting colonial domination. Motivated chiefly by pride and a desire to hold on to the last outpost of what was once the Spanish Empire, Spain's king Alfonso XIII committed Spanish troops to the region in 1909. But the French proved a tough adversary, deal-

Spanish Still Life, *painted by Picasso in 1912, is one of the great works of cubism. Following the lead of 19th-century artists, Picasso and his fellow cubists broke the objects they painted into the most basic geometric forms; they then spread these forms out on the canvas, so that the viewer could see them from all angles.*

ing Spain a series of military setbacks, and a desperate Alfonso was forced to call up reserves from Catalonia.

The separatist and left-leaning Catalans refused to go to war to defend the interests of Spain's landed gentry and the nation's tired, corrupt institutions. Workers in Barcelona, Catalonia's chief city, called a general strike, and there was rioting in the streets for several days before the government put down the revolt. In the course of the street fighting, there were reports of bombings, raids, arrests, tortures, and executions. For example, Francisco Ferrer, an outspoken anarchist leader, was arrested on charges of insurgency. There was a trial, and a good case was made on behalf of Ferrer, but the government was intent on using him as a scapegoat. After Ferrer was found guilty and shot, a wave of liberal sympathy for the martyred anarchist swept the country. In retaliation, anarchists bombed Barcelona's opera house, the Gran Teatre del Liceu, killing 22 people and wounding 50. Santiago Salvador, the anarchist charged with the bombing, was convicted and publicly executed. Violence in the streets intensified as workers—who labored all day for a loaf of bread—and hard-pressed peasants joined with the country's intellectuals to demand social justice by way of political reform.

With Barcelona in turmoil, Picasso and Olivier stayed only briefly in the city, long enough to visit the artist's family and a few friends and to paint *Portrait of Manuel Pallarès.* They traveled to Horta, where Picasso was reunited with the magic of the peasant village he had visited nearly 11 years before.

This second visit to Horta resulted in one of the most productive periods in Picasso's career. He began a series of landscapes, painted several portraits of Olivier, including *Woman with Pears,* and produced a series of still lifes, of which *Still Life with Liqueur Bottle* was the last completed, before he returned to France.

Back in Paris, Picasso and Olivier moved out of Le Bateau Lavoir to 11, boulevard de Clichy. Picasso's paintings were by now selling quite well, so the couple could afford the more comfortable living quarters, which overlooked the tree-lined avenue Frochot. They even hired a maid to do the cooking and serve meals, and they regularly entertained guests. The couple visited Matisse on Fridays and the Steins on Sundays, but mostly Picasso immersed himself in his work. As a result, Olivier began to feel neglected and spent an increasing amount of time with other men.

Picasso barely noticed Olivier's unhappiness. To a large degree, Braque replaced Olivier in Picasso's life. Braque and Picasso visited each other virtually every day, and neither painter considered any canvas finished until the other had passed judgment on it. Picasso's days, his every thought, seemed consumed by his cubist experiments, and this continued until the spring of the following year.

In 1910, Picasso's paintings were exhibited in Budapest, Hungary, at the Galerie Notre-Dame-des-Champs in Paris, at the Grafton Galleries in London, and also in Germany. In June of that year, Picasso and Olivier again vacationed in Spain, this time on the coast of Catalonia, where he produced three etchings illustrating a play by Max Jacob—*Woman with a Mandolin, Nude Woman,* and *The Rower,* all in the high, or extreme, cubist style. Picasso and Olivier returned to Paris in September with a number of unfinished canvases, mostly portraits.

Many critics were horrified by Picasso's paintings and generally by cubism, which under the leadership of Picasso and Braque was increasingly divorced from what painting had been. For example, one critic described Picasso's work as "a return to barbarism and primitive savagery, a repudiation and an utter abasement of all the beauties in life and nature." Another critic, after viewing Picasso's work at an April 1911 New York exhibition, called it "disjointed, disconnected, unrelated, unbeautiful." However, a few more open-minded critics were humbled by Picasso's genius. For instance, in a review that appeared in the *New Age,* John Middleton Murry wrote, "I frankly disclaim any pretension to an understanding or even an appreciation of Picasso. I am awed by him."

In the fall of 1911, Picasso met Eva Gouel, who went by the name Marcelle Humbert, at a gathering hosted by the Steins. A companion of the Polish painter Louis Markus, Humbert began to see Picasso frequently at the Ermitage, one of Picasso's favorite cafés. With his relationship with Olivier fading, Picasso developed an attachment to Humbert; meanwhile, Olivier took up with a young Italian painter named Ubaldo Oppi. It soon became clear that Picasso and Olivier's relationship of seven years was over. That winter, Picasso dedicated his intensely abstract painting *Ma Jolie* to his new lover.

In early 1912, Picasso's paintings were exhibited in Moscow, Munich, and Barcelona. He now had an international reputation, a degree of financial success, and the recognition of his genius by a good many art lovers, dealers, and critics.

Having established himself as one of the world's foremost painters, Picasso began to explore other forms in greater depth. In March 1912 his movement toward synthetic cubism, the three-dimensional counterpart of cubist painting, resulted in *Guitar,* a sculpture made of sheet metal and wire. With this work he broke with the traditional ways of sculpting, namely modeling and carving, and opened the door to a century of constructed sculpture.

In May of that year, Picasso tried a bold experiment: he glued onto a canvas a piece of oilcloth that had been manufactured to look like the caning of a chair seat, and then he painted some other objects,

(*Continued on page 65*)

The Paintings of Pablo Picasso

Two Clowns (1901)

Les Demoiselles d'Avignon (1907)

Self-portrait (1906)

Bottle of Pernod (1911)

Glass, Bouquet, Guitar, and Bottle (1919)

Portrait of Jacqueline with Crossed Hands (1954)

Young Girl Seated (1970)

The Race (1922)

(Continued from page 56)

including a pipe, a knife, a slice of lemon, and a seashell, onto the same canvas. Thus, *Still Life with Chair Caning* was produced. It was the world's first collage, a totally new art form that many other artists would exploit to produce new effects, gluing everything from photographs to newspapers to foil onto canvases. (The word *collage* comes from the French verb *coller,* "to glue.")

Shortly after finishing his first collage, Picasso left on a tour of France that would last some four months. With Humbert, Picasso passed through Céret, Avignon, and Sorgues-sur-l'Ouvèze, returning to Paris in the fall. In October the couple moved into a studio on boulevard Raspail, where Picasso continued his work in two- and three-dimensional forms. Less than a year later, Humbert and Picasso moved again, this time to a studio on rue Schoelcher. Even though their new place was enormous, Picasso's collection of paintings had grown to such proportions that once it was moved into the new studio, little space was left for living.

In 1913, Picasso's work was exhibited in Vienna, Munich, New York, Moscow, Prague, and other major cities around the world to resounding acclaim. By this time he had moved away from analytic cubism into synthetic cubism by synthesizing the fragmented motifs of the former movement into large, flat, colorful shapes that signify objects. *Man with a Guitar,* for example, is a work of synthetic cubism. A work completed in the fall of that year, *Woman in an Armchair,* is an example of a combination of the two forms.

On May 2, Picasso received news that his father was gravely ill. The next day, José Ruiz Blasco was dead. The artist traveled to Barcelona to pay his respects and then returned to France. For the remainder of the year, the grieving Picasso found it difficult to work.

The American author
Gertrude Stein (1874–
1946) in her Paris home.
A friend of Picasso's since
1905, Stein took a keen
interest in his work and
introduced him to other
artists. Picasso's 1906
portrait of Stein, hanging
above her, featured the
African mask motif that
paved the way for the revolutionary Demoiselles.

In August 1914, World War I broke out among the
European powers, pitting France, Great Britain, and
Russia against Germany and Austria-Hungary. In a
burst of patriotic fervor, countless young Frenchmen,
among them Braque and other artists in Picasso's
circle, went off to fight. Because a young, able-bodied
man was a rare sight on the streets of Paris during the
war, Picasso was frequently looked upon with some
suspicion. Many people wondered why he was not off
with the other men of his generation, doing his part
to defeat the Germans. Did he think that because he
was a talented artist that he was above the other young
men who had gone off to risk their lives? Had he no
sense of social responsibility or obligation?

Picasso had mixed feelings about the war. Although he lived in France and had made Paris his

home, he was not French, Spain was neutral, and he had German friends, so his alliances were blurred. Also, Picasso was very much aware of who he was—one of the greatest artists of the 20th century. Deep down he knew that the most valuable contribution he could make to his fellow human beings was through his art, and therefore he may have believed that his life was too valuable to the world for him to risk it on the battlefield, especially when his allegiances were ill defined.

Meanwhile, Humbert had fallen seriously ill. She was coughing up blood and finding it increasingly difficult to breathe. It finally became apparent that what had at first been diagnosed as bronchitis was actually tuberculosis, then a fatal disease. In late 1915, Humbert was hospitalized in Auteuil, a Parisian suburb. Although he visited her regularly, Picasso grew lonely in her absence.

In December, Picasso wrote to Gertrude Stein, who was in Majorca, "My life is hell. Eva becomes more and more ill each day. . . . However, I have made a picture of a Harlequin that, to my way of thinking and to that of many others, is the best thing I have ever done." *Harlequin* is one work in a series of cubist paintings on the harlequin theme that Picasso produced beginning in 1915. The poet Jean Cocteau, on leave from the army, visited Picasso's studio that month with the composer Edgar Varèse, and they may have been among the "many others" who liked the painting.

On December 14, Picasso received the news that his beloved Eva had died. Max Jacob and the painter Juan Gris accompanied him to the funeral. He wrote to Gertrude Stein, telling her how he had been tormented while Eva was suffering and expressing his deep sense of loss now that she was gone. For a period following Gouel's death, Picasso turned inward, seeing very few friends and working little.

Just after Christmas, war-weary Paris was enlivened by a performance of the ballet *Firebird,* by the Russian composer Igor Stravinsky. The dance troupe that performed *Firebird,* the Ballets Russes, was to become famous under the direction of impresario Serge Diaghilev. It was Diaghilev who brought the great dancers Vaslav Nijinsky and Anna Pavlova to Paris and electrified audiences there. Cocteau, one of the century's more creative spirits, was among those delighted by the production and decided to introduce Picasso to the world of ballet. He devised a plan to create a ballet for which French composer Erik Satie would write the music, Picasso would design the costumes and stage sets, and Diaghilev choreographer Léonide Massine would direct the dance. After some shrewd persuasion on the part of Cocteau, the three men began working together. The ballet would be called *Parade.*

Some of his friends at the Café Rotonde tried to discourage Picasso from getting involved in the ballet

Picasso (in cap) poses with stagehands working on the curtain he designed for the ballet Parade, *in 1917. His collaboration on the ballet was merely an interesting sideline in Picasso's career, but it had a major effect on his personal life: during the course of the project he met the ballerina Olga Kokhlova, who soon became his wife.*

project, arguing that it was beneath a man of his talent and stature to design costumes and sets for stage productions. But Picasso was excited about the idea and, characteristically, acted on his instincts. He and Cocteau left for Rome, Italy, where the work would be done.

Picasso derived a certain measure of enthusiasm for the project because of a woman named Olga Kokhlova, one of Diaghilev's ballerinas. The daughter of a colonel in the Imperial Russian Army, Kokhlova had been born in the Ukraine in 1891. She had left home at the age of 21 to join the Ballets Russes, which she was able to do more because of her social status than because of her talent. Although Kokhlova was much more conventional in her background than the women he had known previously, Picasso endowed her with a certain mystery and exotic quality, partly because of his fascination for all things Russian. Picasso did not sweep Kokhlova off her feet, but she found him interesting enough. After all, he was Picasso!

For eight weeks, Picasso threw himself into *Parade,* attending rehearsals and making sketches of the dancers. Quickly these sketches filled his studio, where he had frequent visitors, among them Igor Stravinsky. Picasso and Stravinsky were two of the artistic giants of the 20th century, and when the two men were in the same room, the temperature seemed to rise. Both men had recently shocked the world—Picasso with *Demoiselles* and Stravinsky with *Le Sacre du printemps* (The Rite of Spring), a ballet score that, like Picasso's masterpiece, seemed to summon the passions of some lost pagan era. When the Diaghilev troupe left for performances in Naples in March and Florence in April, Picasso and Stravinsky went along and spent a good deal of time together walking the streets of the beautiful Italian cities.

Parade opened on May 18, 1917, at the Théâtre du Châtelet and outraged the audience. The curtain rose to the blaring of sirens, trains, planes, and other noises that make up daily life in the 20th century. Picasso had naturally thought that since the performance would take place less than 200 miles from where French soldiers were being slaughtered by German artillery, *Parade* should shatter all the conventions of ballet. And it did: Picasso's costumes and sets mocked, even insulted, the traditions the French audience had come to expect from a night at the ballet. The theater resounded with boos and hisses, and some in the audience shouted insults and cursed Picasso's name.

The critic Apollinaire had a different view. He wrote that Picasso and Massine

> consummated for the first time this marriage of painting and dance, of plastic art to mime that is the sign of the accession to the throne of a more complete art. . . . This new alliance—for until now costume and decor on the one hand, choreography on the other, have been linked only artificially—has resulted in *Parade* in a kind of surrealism which I see as the point of departure for a series of manifestations of the new spirit.

Juan Gris also praised the performance, calling it "unpretentious, gay, and distinctly comic."

But most critics were offended by *Parade.* One in particular used such strong language to criticize the work that Erik Satie saw fit to respond to him in an equally abusive letter. The critic then sued Satie for libel and defamation of character, and the composer was eventually sentenced to a week in jail. *Parade,* with all the outrage, uproar, and scandal surrounding it, was the first modern work of performance art. Initially condemned as a work of the devil that made a mockery of all that is sacred in art, *Parade* was eventually recognized as a modern masterpiece. The offstage drama meant nothing to Picasso, who knew full well what he was doing and mostly ignored criticism.

Among Picasso's greatest friends and admirers was the French poet Guillaume Apollinaire, shown here during his recovery from a serious head wound suffered in World War I. When audiences and critics savagely attacked Parade, *Apollinaire defended the ballet as an example of "the new spirit."*

The dance troupe traveled to Spain in June, and Picasso followed, but when the troupe left for South America, he and Kokhlova stayed in Barcelona, where he was given a homecoming celebration by some of his fellow painters. While there, he painted *Olga Picasso in a Mantilla,* a painting done in the naturalistic style at Kokhlova's request. She had asked him to make her face recognizable in the portrait. Also while in Barcelona, Picasso introduced Kokhlova to his mother, who advised the dancer against marrying her son.

Kokhlova did not take María Picasso's advice. She and Picasso were married on July 12, 1918, at the Russian Orthodox church on rue Daru in Paris. Jacob, Cocteau, Apollinaire, Diaghilev, Massine, Matisse, Braque, and Gertrude Stein were among the luminaries in attendance. Then the newlyweds were off to the seashore resort Biarritz for their honeymoon.

On November 9, Picasso was shaving in his bathroom in Paris when he heard the news of the death of his friend Apollinaire, a victim of the lethal influenza pandemic that was sweeping the globe. The news shocked him; Apollinaire was only 39 years old and for some 14 years had been one of the artist's closest friends. Two days after the death of Apollinaire, World War I ended. Many celebrated the end of the killing; some wept over the many lives lost in the war, which had shattered the hopes and dreams of a generation. Picasso, a solitary figure on the landscape and yet somehow a personification of the times, sank into a deep malaise.

THE BULL AND THE TYRANTS

During the 1920s, Paris was a teeming cultural mecca. Countless painters, writers, musicians, and intellectuals flocked there from all over the world to work, share ideas, and perhaps achieve success. The great Irish writer James Joyce was there, as were the American novelists Ernest Hemingway and F. Scott Fitzgerald. Many who arrived in Paris were not writers or artists at all; eccentric millionaires, bohemians, and political refugees went to Paris as well, simply because it was *the* place to be for those who lived on the fringe of mainstream society. At her home, Gertrude Stein hosted many artistic luminaries and other members of what she referred to as "the lost generation."

On January 18, 1920, the Romanian intellectual and expatriate Tristan Tzara arrived in Paris at the invitation of the French writers André Breton and Louis Aragon. Together with Philippe Soupault, the poet Paul Éluard, and other writers, they began a movement called dadaism (also known as Dada) and published the magazine *Littérature,* the movement's principal vehicle. Although Tzara once explained that dadaism was actually conceived at the Cabaret Voltaire in Zurich, Switzerland, in 1916, it was his arrival in Paris and his collaboration with these other writers and intellectuals—with whom he shared a deep revul-

Picasso during the 1920s, photographed by the surrealist artist Man Ray. In the course of the decade, Picasso moved away from cubism and experimented with surrealism; with the same restless spirit, he also sought new departures in his emotional life.

sion for virtually everything art had become—that gave birth to the dadaist movement.

The dadaists proclaimed the bankruptcy of art, which they believed had been corrupted by centuries of bogus refinement and artifice. They maintained that art must represent life and reality as one experiences it—a random, nonsensical, meaningless bombardment of sounds and images in an empty, godless universe—and that the only real art is the expression of or indulgence in individual whim. In the early 1920s, many dadaists declared the death of cubism, but Tzara was not among those who did. He wrote, "As long as there are painters like Picasso, Braque, and Gris . . . no one can speak of the death of cubism without sounding like an idiot." In truth, although Picasso and others continued to use cubist techniques, the dadaists were correct in their pronouncement in that cubism was no longer a viable artistic movement after 1920.

Although cubism reached its fullest development from 1911 to 1918, even during this period one can trace in Picasso's work a movement away from the cubist style. As Gertrude Stein wrote, as early as 1914, "there were less cubes in cubism." By the early 1920s, Picasso, although still producing cubist paintings and sculptures, increasingly worked in other styles as well. For example, *Two Seated Women,* which he did in 1920, *Three Women at the Spring,* a work he produced in 1921, and *The Bathers,* also from 1921, are in a neoclassic style. Although Picasso loved to discuss painting and obviously understood a lot about theories of painting, he did not give much importance to intellectual theorizing about art. "Everyone wants to understand art," he once complained. "Why not try to understand the songs of a bird? Why does one love the night, flowers, everything around us, without trying to understand them? But in the case of painting people have to *understand.* If only they would realize above all that an artist works of necessity."

In 1921, Olga Picasso gave birth to a baby boy, Paulo, and Pablo documented his son's first months in a series of sketches. By now Picasso enjoyed tremendous international success. Not only were his paintings fetching very high prices; he had continued his work with Diaghilev's Ballets Russes, designing and creating costumes and sets for several ballets, and cubism had become a movement of vast proportions. He was now earning more than 1 million francs a year and frequently attended exclusive parties thrown by Parisian high society. During the summer of 1921, Pablo, Olga, and baby Paulo moved into an impressive villa in Fontainebleau, where Picasso painted the two well-known versions of *Three Musicians.* But the painter quickly grew tired of the domestic world of clipped shrubbery, clean, spacious rooms, and servants in the suburbs. His relationship with his wife had also become strained. In September, he moved his family back to Paris, clearly looking for a new direction for his life and art.

In Paris, as dadaism dissipated into the nothingness from which it came, surrealism took its place. Breton, who had parted with Tzara and had met the Austrian psychoanalyst Sigmund Freud in 1921, became the leader of the surrealist movement, which emphasized the artistic exploration of dreams and the human subconscious, both central subjects of Freud's work. Breton had met Picasso in 1918, greatly admired the painter's work, and wrote about it in *Littérature.* In 1922, he and Aragon persuaded a French art collector to purchase Picasso's *Les Demoiselles.* By 1925, when he was represented in a Paris exhibition entitled "La Peinture Surréaliste," Picasso had one foot firmly planted in the surrealist school.

Meanwhile, Picasso's other foot was feeling for new terrain, particularly in his personal life. He had grown restless, bored with his relationship with Olga and their life together. Thus, it is not surprising that in

In The Three Musicians, *painted in 1921, Picasso bridges the gap between cubism and surrealism. The painting exhibits the geometric patterns of cubism but also evokes the whimsical and dreamlike canvases of the surrealists.*

January 1927, when he saw the beautiful Marie-Thérèse Walter as she emerged from the Métro (the Paris subway) near the Galeries Lafayette (a famous Parisian department store), Picasso stepped up and introduced himself. "Mademoiselle, you have an interesting face. I would like to make your portrait. I am Picasso."

The name meant nothing to Walter, who was 17 years old, some 30 years younger than Picasso, and knew nothing of him or the art world. But Picasso was eager to teach her, and she found him irresistible. They met again two days later, and they talked and went to a movie. He courted her for about six months, and they became lovers on her 18th birthday, but Picasso kept the affair a secret.

In the late 1920s, Picasso continued to explore surrealistic themes. For example, during the summer of 1927 he executed an album of pen-and-ink drawings called *The Metamorphoses,* and in the fall he painted *Seated Woman* and began his exploration of the Minotaur theme, all in the surrealist style. In 1929,

Picasso began working on a large metal sculpture entitled *Woman in a Garden* and painted *Bust of a Woman with Self-Portrait* and *Woman Bather on the Beach,* marking the beginning of a period (lasting several months) in which he portrayed women as aggressive and even monstrous beings.

During the early 1930s, Picasso enjoyed increasing success. His work continued to be reproduced in important art magazines and journals such as *Minotaure,* a surrealist magazine, the first issue of which was published in May 1933. It had a Picasso Minotaur on its cover and included reproductions of a number of Picasso's works. Picasso's work was also exhibited at the world's most prestigious art galleries, including the Reinhardt, John Becker, and Valentine galleries in New York; Galerie Goëmans and Galeries Georges Petit in Paris; the Arts Club of Chicago; and in a major retrospective, "Thirty Years of Pablo Picasso," at the gallery Alex Reid & Lefèvre in London. Also during this time, Marie-Thérèse Walter began to figure more prominently in Picasso's work. For example, in early 1932, Picasso painted a series of sleeping women for

A Man Ray photograph of Picasso, dressed as a bullfighter, and his wife, Olga (right), at a 1920s costume ball. Internationally acclaimed and increasingly wealthy, Picasso now had access to the world of high society and stately homes; but his eyes betray the volcanic energy that was soon to shatter his peaceful family life.

which she was the model, and in 1933 he began a series of etchings, later known as the Vollard Suite, for which he also used her.

That year, another woman who had figured prominently in his life reentered Picasso's world. When he returned from a vacation in Spain, Picasso was dismayed to discover that Fernande Olivier had published excerpts from her memoirs in *Le Soir* and the *Mercure de France.* Olivier was working as a teacher and decided to publish an account of her association with the great artist whose life and hard times she had shared some 20 years before. Not wanting such an intimate glimpse into his personal life to appear in print, Picasso sought to block the publication of the memoirs. Olga Picasso also wanted her husband's past affairs to receive as little publicity as possible. But notwithstanding Picasso's efforts, the memoirs were eventually published under the title *Picasso and His Friends.* The book was not hostile, but this mattered very little to Picasso, who wanted to control and define the legend that surrounded his name. For a time he took out his frustrations on Olga and Marie-Thérèse; then, in August 1934, he returned briefly with his family to Spain, where his marriage continued to fray at the edges.

In his work from this period, Picasso continued to explore the theme of the mythical Minotaur, a powerful, violent beast and for him a symbol of defiance and destruction. The etchings of the period, which include *Bull Goring a Horse, Dying Bull, Death of the Toreador,* and *Bull Disemboweling a Horse,* attest to the rage Picasso was feeling at the time and the great degree to which he identified with the plight of the beast. Like a bull in a ring, Picasso was tormented by the frustrating confines of his marriage and was desperately looking for a chance to break free. To make matters worse, he was finding little consolation in the company of his lover. And he was about to find the walls of the ring closing in on him even further; Marie-Thérèse Walter was pregnant.

Upon hearing this news, Olga Picasso took Paulo, left her husband, and moved into a hotel room nearby. Picasso welcomed the separation, but he knew a divorce settlement under French law would likely mean his having to part not only with half his money but also with many of his paintings. This was one reason he had not sought a divorce himself much earlier. He continued to hope he could avoid the ordeal.

On September 5, 1935, Walter gave birth to a baby girl, María de la Concepción, named after Picasso's sister, who died as a child. Picasso was pleased to have

Marie-Thérèse Walter, photographed in 1927, the year she met Picasso. Walter and Picasso, who was 30 years her senior, became lovers on her 18th birthday; when Walter gave birth to a daughter, María de la Concepción, in 1935, the event put an end to Picasso's marriage.

a daughter, but his romance with Walter no longer possessed the vitality it once had, and he began to think about leaving her.

Picasso fell into a period in which he painted very little but wrote a great deal. He made long entries in his journal, wrote letters, and even composed poems. Picasso's poetry was in stream of consciousness, the so-called automatic style of the surrealists. He also spent a great deal of time with his childhood friend Jaime Sabartès, who moved into Picasso's apartment on rue La Boëtie, and with Paul Éluard, who was quickly becoming one of Picasso's closest friends. But these men could not rescue Picasso from the torment he was feeling; he would have to take care of his own problems before he could return to his work.

In early 1936, another beautiful young woman stirred Picasso's passions. Her name was Dora Maar, shortened from Henriette Theodora Markovitch. Picasso was introduced to her by Éluard at the Deux-Magots, a café frequented by surrealists. Half Yugoslav and half French, Maar was a photographer, a painter, and a genuine intellectual; having lived in Argentina for a time, she also spoke fluent Spanish. A regular at the Deux-Magots, she was a close friend of Breton's. Unlike Marie-Thérèse Walter, Maar was sophisticated and could discuss art and philosophy with the painters and thinkers of the day. Picasso was immediately intrigued.

That year, Picasso's work was included in numerous exhibitions around the world, including a major show called "Cubism and Abstract Art," at the Museum of Modern Art in New York. He began to work furiously, completing the painting *Sleeping Woman Before Green Shutters,* for which he used Walter as a model, and he began a series of drawings and watercolors in which he returned to the theme of the Minotaur.

As Picasso concentrated on his work in his studio, the world around him was changing rapidly. In June a new government—a coalition of middle-class liberals, Socialists, and Communists, known as the Popular Front—was elected in France. In Spain, a related party, also called the Popular Front, had won handily in elections held in February, but the military and right-wing elements, led by the Fascist Francisco Franco, had moved to hold on to power by force. When supporters of the new Spanish Republic took to the streets to reclaim their country, they clashed with Franco's Nationalists, and blood ran in the streets. By midyear, Spain was embroiled in a full-scale civil war.

Although he was spending long days closed up in his studio engrossed in his work, Picasso did not remain aloof from the political turmoil around him and in his native Spain. In early summer he honored Léon Blum, the leader of the Popular Front in France and that country's first Socialist premier, by agreeing to lend a design to adorn the drop curtain for a performance of Romain Rolland's *14 Juillet* at the Alhambra Theater on Independence Day. Picasso was also vocal about his support for the Republicans in Spain and his opposition to Franco, who was quickly positioning himself to take control of Spain.

Franco had powerful supporters. For example, affluent Spanish landowners looked to a Franco regime as their best chance of holding on to their wealth, and U.S. and British business leaders made handsome profits from selling oil and trucks to Franco's Nationalists. The most infamous among Franco's supporters were the Fascist dictators Benito Mussolini of Italy and Adolf Hitler of Germany. When Franco needed help transporting his Army of Africa from Morocco to north-central Spain, where the insurgent general Emilio Mola Vidal had declared a provisional Nationalist government under his own leadership, he turned to Mussolini and Hitler. Believing a Fascist Spain would fit well with their plans to conquer Europe, they agreed to send not only transport planes but artillery as well.

On October 1, 1936, Franco declared himself head of the Spanish government, but despite the ruthless measures carried out by his military police, his power was by no means consolidated. Not only did he still face the opposition of General Mola and his army of some 20,000 men—the Republican resistance also stood in Franco's way. Moreover, the International Brigades, men from all over the world who had vol- unteered to go to Spain to stop the spread of fascism, fought on the side of the Republic. Still, Franco was confident that with the help of Mussolini and Hitler he would soon conquer Spain for the Nationlist cause.

But Mussolini and Hitler were becoming impa-tient with Franco and threatened to throw their sup-port behind Mola Vidal. They were interested in a Fascist Spain and cared little who presided over it. They decided to step up their efforts to secure Spain for the Nationalists and launched a bombing cam-paign over Madrid, a stronghold of democratic resis-tance. In November, Nationalist forces attacked the Republican militia positioned at the entrance to Ma-drid, opened fire on citizens in the streets, and marched down the city's main thoroughfares, murder-ing those who stood in their way. From above, Ger-man planes joined Nationalist bombers in a daily assault on the city's civilian neighborhoods.

The contempt Picasso had for Franco is evident in his January 1937 etching *Dream and Lie of Franco,* in which the general is depicted as a grotesque buffoon. Appreciative of the artist's condemnation of Franco's rebellion, the Republicans invited Picasso to serve as director of Spain's Prado Museum and in early 1937 invited him to paint a mural for the Spanish Pavilion at the Paris World's Fair, scheduled to open in June.

Picasso's relaxed pose at his home in Mougins, France, in 1936 belies the turmoil surrounding him. His involvement with a new flame, Dora Maar, had further complicated his personal life; in the political sphere, the Fascist assault on the Spanish Republic deeply distressed him.

As war raged on in Madrid, Franco turned his attention to the liberal factions in the Basque Provinces in the north, which presented him with another obstacle to his domination of Spain. On April 26, 1937, a savage bombing campaign was launched on the Basque village of Guernica. The raid lasted only three hours, but nearly a quarter of the town's 7,000 inhabitants were killed in the bloody slaughter, which stunned the international community and brought Franco worldwide condemnation. When he saw shocking photos taken of the village in the aftermath of the bombing, Picasso threw himself into his work. The title of his mural for the Spanish Pavilion would be *Guernica*.

CHAPTER SIX

LABORS AND LOVES

Rare are those solitary figures in history who through an act of sublime compassion rise above the blinding, burning dust of disaster to inspire those who would muster the courage to begin anew. Through the centuries, senseless tragedy has weighed heavily on individual lives, causing the wheels of human progress to slip badly, and with its penchant for avarice and hostility, humanity has brought much suffering on itself. But the human race has always found the strength to sustain itself and to strive for a better way of life for everyone. Those who have had their turn at the wheel have not always navigated with wisdom, but through the centuries there have always been those who wrestled with the current to steer civilization through the dark fog of greed and hatred toward a brighter future. Picasso was such a person.

A passionately driven Picasso went to work on the *Guernica* mural, making more than 50 study sketches incorporating some of his familiar themes, including the Minotaur and images from the *Dream and Lie of Franco*. He worked day and night, and within weeks one of the great masterpieces of the 20th century began to take form. The artist allowed certain people to come to his studio and watch him work, and Dora Maar, whose own political vision and conviction fueled Picasso's rage and added to the work, docu-

Picasso making pottery in his studio at Vallauris, France. When Picasso and his new love, Françoise Gilot, moved to Vallauris in 1948, the artist devoted his creative energies to reviving the town's ceramics industry—a year later, 149 pieces of Vallauris pottery went on exhibition in Paris.

mented the progress of *Guernica* by photographing it in stages. The Spanish artist was determined to condemn violence in the most powerful way possible. For Picasso, the artistic genius of his age, that way was to create a violent, horrifying masterwork that would depict the brutality of Guernica's martyrdom and the debasement of life and beauty that was fascism.

As if the work did not speak loudly enough, Picasso issued an emphatic statement of his position on Franco and the Spanish Civil War. He wrote, "The Spanish struggle is the fight of reaction against the people, against freedom. . . . In the panel on which I am working, which I shall call *Guernica,* and in all my recent works of art, I clearly express my abhorrence of the military caste which has sunk Spain in an ocean of pain and death." In early June, *Guernica,* a huge canvas that measured $11\frac{1}{2}$ by $25\frac{1}{2}$ feet, was installed in the Spanish Pavilion at the Paris World's Fair.

That summer, Picasso and Dora Maar traveled to Mougins, where they met Paul Éluard and his wife, Nusch. They also went to Nice to visit Matisse, who had moved there in 1916. They traveled with Picasso's dog, Kazbek, and cases of brushes and paints. Marie-Thérèse Walter, however, did not go along; she was slowly being edged out of Picasso's life.

Picasso's work was exhibited at several retrospective shows in 1937. In November, 23 of his pieces were presented in a New York show entitled "Picasso from 1901 to 1937." The show included *Les Demoiselles d'Avignon,* which soon after was purchased by the Museum of Modern Art for $24,000. Other major exhibits of his work that year included "Fifty Drawings by Pablo Picasso" and "Chirico and Picasso," both at the Zwemmer Gallery in London.

Picasso's deep concern for the Republican cause in Spain prompted him to address the American Artists' Congress in New York in December 1937. Franco had publicly accused the Republican government in Spain of mistreating the country's priceless art treasures. Picasso, as director of the Prado, issued a statement, published in the *New York Times,* in which he rejected Franco's propaganda and defended the Republican government against the charge. He said, "The democratic government of the Spanish Republic has taken all the necessary measures to protect the artistic treasures of Spain during this cruel and unjust war." And he went on to drive home a theme about which he felt very strongly and one he would return to repeatedly later in his life. "Artists cannot and should not," he said, "remain indifferent to a conflict in which the highest values of humanity and civilization are at stake."

Meanwhile, fascism was steadily on the rise, and the world watched in fear. In March 1938, German troops entered and occupied Austria, and in September the leaders of France, Great Britain, Germany, and Italy signed the Munich Pact, delivering Czechoslovakia to Hitler. On January 26, 1939, the Fascists seized Barcelona, where tens of thousands of lives were lost in battle, and on March 26 they took Madrid. On April 1, the Spanish Civil War came to an end. Franco had won an unconditional victory, and about a half million people fled Spain. When Franco announced the Law of Political Responsibilities, a proclamation under which returning refugees would be tried and executed, some 400,000 Spanish refugees remained in France rather than return to their homeland, where they would be likely to face the death squads. But Franco had his executions anyway; from 1936 to 1944, some 400,000 Spaniards were killed on his orders.

Meanwhile, the rise of fascism in Europe met little resistance. German forces marched on Prague, Czechoslovakia, in March 1939, and on September 1 they invaded Poland. Two days later, Great Britain and

France (the Allies) declared war on Germany, beginning World War II. That year, a major retrospective, "Picasso: Forty Years of His Art," took place at New York's Museum of Modern Art. The show consisted of more than 300 pieces of Picasso's work, including *Guernica,* his bold anti-Fascist mural, and many of the studies he did for it.

In May 1940, Germany invaded Belgium and crossed the border into France. Anticipating a German march on Paris, Picasso fled the city with Dora Maar, settling in the town of Royan. The Germans entered Paris in June, and the French premier Henri Pétain and Hitler signed an armistice, which essentially surrendered French sovereignty to the Germans. Later that month the Germans entered Royan virtually uncontested, and Picasso returned to his Paris studio on rue des Grands-Augustins, where he stayed throughout the German occupation of France. German officers would sometimes drop in on him there, and Picasso would sardonically give them souvenir picture postcards of *Guernica.* Picasso later told the story of how when one officer looked at his postcard and asked Picasso "Did you do this?" the artist responded, "No, you did."

Eventually, Picasso was regularly harassed by the German occupiers. A good many of his works, which the Nazis declared "degenerate," were confiscated, and some were badly damaged. The Nazis also forbade anyone to exhibit Picasso's work. He received invitations to take up residence in the United States and Mexico, but he was determined to stay in Paris, where he had his work, his family, his friends, and the most creative atmosphere he had ever known, despite the Nazi presence. Throughout 1940, he continued painting, writing, and tending to his now quite extended family. His son, Paulo, was in school in neutral Switzerland, but Picasso stayed in touch with his wife,

Picasso poses with a sculpture in his Paris studio in November 1944. During the Nazi occupation, Picasso was allowed to remain in Paris, but his work was banned from public view. After the liberation of Paris in August 1944, Picasso reemerged with an exhibition of 50 new paintings and sculptures in the Salon d'Automne.

Olga, to get news of the boy, and he visited Marie-Thérèse Walter and his daughter on weekends.

During the early 1940s, Picasso began a series of drawings that would result in the large sculpture *Man with Sheep.* He also painted *Portrait of Dora Maar* and returned to creating three-dimensional canvases. For example, for *The Flowering Watering Can,* done in 1943, he mounted an actual watering can on the canvas. For *Head of a Bull,* from the same year, Picasso mounted an old bicycle saddle and handlebars to depict his subject matter.

In May of that year, Picasso met the young painter Françoise Gilot at a Paris restaurant, where she and her friend Geneviève Aliquot were at a table with some others. Picasso brought her a bowl of cherries and invited both young women, who boldly declared their artistic ambitions to the great master, to visit his studio the following day. They accepted and arrived at Picasso's studio the next morning to find him in the company of several people and too busy to spend much time with them. But they were invited back, and after that day, Gilot visited the studio alone regularly. Picasso took an active interest in her painting. He was 62, and she was 22 years old—a generational chasm rarely bridged by romantic love—but the possibility was clearly there for both of them. He gave her tubes of paint and instruction in etching. Soon she was appearing in his drawings, and Dora Maar was slowly painted out of the picture.

Meanwhile, the Nazis continued their terror campaign across Europe. One of the main concerns of Nazi ideology was to rid the world of groups of people the Third Reich considered inferior, in order to make a "pure" race. Thus, many groups of people—including Jews, Gypsies, the disabled, homosexuals, and political and religious dissidents—were gassed, hanged, shot, or more gradually killed by forced labor, medical experimentation, exposure, or starvation. In all, 11.5 million persons were killed. The Nazis particularly targeted Jews. In Germany and the occupied countries, Jews were required to wear yellow Stars of David on their clothing so that they could be readily identified. Later, the authorities systematically rounded up Jews and placed them in concentration camps. Picasso saw a number of his friends—Max Jacob and the writer Robert Desnos, for example—incarcerated by the Nazis in 1944, and mostly out of fear he made no effort to use his considerable influence on their behalf.

In March of that year, a reading of a play Picasso had written, *Le Désir attrapé par la queue* (*Desire Caught by the Tail*), was staged by a talented group of French writers and actors. It was directed by the great novelist and essayist Albert Camus. Among the readers were the philosopher, novelist, playwright, and founder of the French existentialist movement, Jean-Paul Sartre; Sartre's longtime companion, the writer Simone de Beauvoir; and the novelist Raymond Queneau. The audience included Braque and the masterful Hungarian photographer Brassaï, among others.

That summer, the German occupiers clashed increasingly with units of the French Resistance, an underground network of French patriots who refused to surrender their country to Hitler. By this time the United States and the Soviet Union had joined the Allies in their effort to thwart the German campaign, and members of the Resistance were encouraged by the all-out Allied effort to liberate Europe from the grip of fascism. Allied forces had landed on the coast of Normandy in June, and by August they had reached Paris. Then, on August 25, Allied troops liberated Paris from the Germans, and the city rejoiced with music and champagne.

About a month after the liberation of Paris, Picasso joined the Communist party, and the news was made public on October 5 in *L'Humanité,* the official party newspaper. In an interview published in the paper, Picasso explained why he joined the Communists:

> Joining the Communist Party is the logical conclusion of my whole life, my whole work. . . . I have always been an exile, now I no longer am; until the day when Spain can welcome me back, the French Communist Party opened its arms to me, and I have found in it those that I most value, the greatest scientists, the greatest poets, all those beautiful faces of Parisian insurgents that I saw during the August days; I am once more among my brothers.

Picasso has been roundly criticized for joining the Communist party, which after all was the party of Joseph Stalin, the Soviet dictator who ordered the murder of his political opponents and who imposed harsh policies that caused millions of peasants to starve during the 1930s. But Picasso, like so many writers, artists, and intellectuals of the time, was attracted to the ideals of communism—a more even distribution of wealth, an end to the exploitation of working people and peasants by the wealthy, a government ruled by the working class, and an economy driven by cooperation and common ownership rather than by competition—and he had witnessed legions of Communists fight and dic in the struggle against facism.

During the mid- and late 1940s, Picasso's work continued to reflect his revulsion from the absurd and widespread violence of his time. In 1945, he gave his energies to painting a second antiwar canvas, *The Charnel House,* and a series of still lifes, including *Still Life with Skull, Leek, and Pottery,* that stress the tragedy of war, the terror of the German occupation, and the horror of the Nazi concentration camps. In April of that year, U.S. troops entered the Nazi concentration camp at Dachau, and shortly thereafter photographs attesting to the atrocities that took place there were published in newspapers around the world.

Françoise Gilot moved in with Picasso the following year, and she modeled regularly for him. She gave birth to the couple's first son, Claude, in May 1947, and in 1948 they moved to a villa in the hills above Vallauris, in southeastern France, where Picasso devoted his energies to revitalizing the town's ceramics industry, which had been in decline since World War I. (Vallauris was the home of Madoura pottery, made in the shop of the master potter Georges Ramié.) Picasso's work that year culminated in a November

Donning a toreador's cap, Picasso presides at a mock bullfight in Vallauris in 1955. Though in his early seventies, the artist showed no signs of slowing down; he continued to work at a furious pace and to pursue the possibilities of romance.

exhibition of 149 ceramics at the Maison de la Pensée Française in Paris. In April 1949, Gilot gave birth again, this time to a daughter, Paloma. Picasso took a great deal of pleasure in his young children, and they were often the subject of his work. In January 1950 he painted *Claude and Paloma* and *Claude and Paloma at Play.*

Despite his work and family obligations, Picasso remained politically committed and active during the 1950s. In October 1950 he attended the Second World Peace Conference in Sheffield, England, and the poster commemorating the event bore an image of a dove taken from a Picasso lithograph. That year he won the Lenin Peace Prize. The following year he painted *Massacre in Korea,* his statement against U.S. intervention in that country, and in 1952 he began plans to decorate a 14th-century chapel in Vallauris as a temple of peace. For this project, Picasso painted two large panels, one on war and one on peace.

By the mid–1950s, Picasso's relationship with Gilot was terribly strained, and she had moved back to Paris with the children. In April 1954, Picasso met a young model named Sylvette David, and in a month's time he completed some 40 drawings and oils of her. He then took up with a pottery seller in her late twenties named Jacqueline Roque, whom he had met the previous summer in Vallauris. She was recently divorced and had a six-year-old daughter, Catherine. In September of that year she moved into his Grands-Augustins studio. The following year, Picasso executed a number of works for which Roque posed, including *Jacqueline in a Turkish Vest* and a portrait of her based on a painting by the French painter Edouard Manet.

In 1958, Picasso bought and took up residence at Château de Vauvenargues, a 14th-century estate near Aix-en-Provence.

There he painted variations on great masterworks, particularly nudes and bathers by Manet. He also returned to the theme of the artist and the model, one he would focus on continually for the next 10 years. In 1960 a major retrospective of Picasso's work was presented from July through September at the Tate Gallery in London. Organized by the Arts Council of Great Britain, the show contained 270 pieces. Meanwhile, Picasso continued to paint and to sculpt at an amazing pace, completing more than 20 canvases, a large-scale sheet-metal sculpture, and several maquettes, made from cut and folded paper and cardboard.

On March 2, 1961, Picasso and Jacqueline Roque were married at Vallauris Town Hall. (His former wife, Olga, had died in 1955.) Picasso and Jacqueline soon moved into a new villa, Notre-Dame-de-Vie, near Mougins and overlooking Cannes. The incredibly energetic artist celebrated his 80th birthday that October and showed no signs of slowing down, either in his labors or his loves.

ROMANTIC WARRIOR

Although his work continued to be shown in smaller galleries, such as the Galerie Louise Leris in Paris, by the early 1960s Picasso had completed such an enormous body of work that very large exhibitions were commonplace around the world, and his life was a constant shower of accolades. For example, "Picasso: An American Tribute" opened in April 1962. It was a cooperative exhibition in which 309 works were shown at nine New York galleries. The following month, the Museum of Modern Art presented "Picasso 80th Birthday Exhibition: The Museum Collection, Present and Future." The Museo Picasso, in Barcelona, opened its doors in March 1963, and that same year, Picasso accepted a commission to execute a 60-foot sculpture for Chicago's new Civic Center. In January of the following year, the retrospective "Picasso and Man" opened at the Art Gallery of Toronto in Canada. Consisting of 273 works from the period 1898–1961, the exhibit ran through the middle of February before being moved to Montreal for a month. In May, a major Picasso retrospective was presented at the National Museum of Modern Art in Tokyo, Japan, through July, and Brassaï's book *Conver-*

sations avec Picasso was published by Gallimard. (The book was later published in English under the title *Picasso and Company.*)

One tribute, if it can be called one, that Picasso was not happy with was the publication of Françoise Gilot's reminiscences under the title *Life with Picasso,* in 1964. The book does not present Picasso in an entirely negative light, although Gilot does characterize him as an egomaniacal genius and somewhat emotionally immature. But Picasso cared little whether the book was complimentary; he objected to it mainly because he felt the subject of his relationship with the author was too intimate for popular consumption. He also preferred to maintain control over his own public image.

Desperate to stop the serialization of the book in the magazine *Paris-Match,* Picasso turned to the French courts, calling the work "an intolerable intrusion" into his private life. However, the courts refused to issue an order blocking the serialization. Picasso then brought an action against Calmann-Lévy, the publisher of the book in France, and asked the court to ban the book, but the case was dismissed. Refusing to give up, the artist filed an appeal, which was supported by 40 of the most prominent French artists and intellectuals of the day. In the end, the appeals court ruled that "intimacy does not belong exclusively to either lover." Just as Picasso had exercised his right to paint Gilot, she had the right to portray him as she knew him. Picasso's appeal was rejected, and the book was published.

Through the early 1960s, the artist continued to experiment and innovate, all the while creating more works than many artists less than half his age. In 1962 alone, he executed more than 100 engravings, among other pieces, and in 1964 he completed a model for the Civic Center sculpture based on his 1962 metalwork *Head of a Woman.* But in 1965, Picasso's health began to fail. He was hospitalized in November of that year at the American Hospital in Neuilly and underwent gallbladder and prostate surgery. He gave up smoking during his convalescence.

Meanwhile, the tributes continued. In November 1966, a huge Picasso exhibition opened in Paris. Under the direction of the French writer André Malraux, who was now the French minister of cultural affairs, the major retrospective was presented by the French government and included more than 700 works. Paintings were exhibited at the Grand Palais; drawings,

The welded steel sculpture Head of a Woman, *completed in 1964, shows Picasso's tireless interest in experimenting with forms and techniques. His physical energy was equally remarkable: in 1962 alone, at the age of 81, he had completed more than 100 engravings.*

sculptures, and ceramics at the Petit Palais; and prints at France's national library, the Bibliothèque Nationale. The following year, the Tate Gallery in London presented a major exhibition of Picasso's sculptures and ceramics. The show ran from October through the end of the year.

As the decade drew to a close, Picasso's physical powers were clearly waning. Although he made 347 engravings during the period from February through March 1968 and continued to paint, his friends knew he was coming to the end of his life. After all, he was nearly 90 years old. But Picasso insisted he was feeling fine and said, "You know, you must never equate age with death. The one has nothing to do with the other."

During the early 1970s, the numerous Picasso retrospectives presented around the world seemed to anticipate the end of the artist's long and prolific life. In January 1970, the Picasso family in Barcelona donated all the paintings and sculptures in its possession to the Museo Picasso. In October of that year, the exhibition "Picasso: Master Printmaker" opened at the Museum of Modern Art in New York, and in December "The Cubist Epoch" opened in Los Angeles. The Los Angeles exhibition was moved to New York's Metropolitan Museum of Art in 1971. That same year, New Yorkers flocked to the Museum of Modern Art to see an exhibition of the Gertrude Stein collection, which included 38 works by Picasso. William Rubin, the Museum of Modern Art's chief curator, met with Picasso to discuss a major exhibition and a related book. On October 25, 1971, an exhibition of Picasso's work opened in the Grand Gallery of the Louvre, in Paris, to honor the artist on his 90th birthday. And finally, in January 1972, the exhibit organized by Rubin, "Picasso in the Collection of the Museum of Modern Art," opened in New York.

Picasso continued working, producing mainly drawings and prints. He executed 156 etchings between January 1970 and March 1972. In the fall of 1972, the artist was admitted to the hospital with severe pulmonary congestion, and rumors of Picasso's impending death swept Paris. But the rumors were somewhat premature. In early 1973 he painted *Character with a Bird*, a variation on Rembrandt's *Falconer*. During the first days of April, he wrote to Marie-Thérèse Walter, telling her that she was the only woman he had ever loved.

But on April 8, 1973, the great Pablo Picasso could hold on no longer. His doctor was summoned, but there was little he could do to prolong the artist's life. He massaged his patient's chest, and for a few hours Picasso struggled for breath. He called out to Jacqueline, who was at his side. Finally, his heart failed at 11:45 that morning, and he was gone.

Anything that can be said about Picasso pales in comparison to what he said himself through his work. He left behind some 50,000 works of art, including 1,885 paintings; 1,228 sculptures; 2,880 ceramics; 18,095 engravings; 6,112 lithographs; and approximately 12,000 drawings, as well as numerous linocuts, tapestries, and rugs, not to mention his letters, poetry, and plays. Even a small fraction of this enormous body of work would be enough to establish Picasso as one of the artistic geniuses of his day and no doubt one of the most revolutionary artists ever to put a brush to canvas.

Picasso stands alongside the 20th century's most brilliant creators—his friend the painter Henri Matisse; literary greats James Joyce, William Faulkner, Franz Kafka, T. S. Eliot, and Samuel Beckett; the philosopher Jean-Paul Sartre; composers Igor Stravinsky, Arnold Schönberg, and Béla Bartók; and the renowned physicist Albert Einstein—and like them, through his work he will live forever. The 20th century relied on the vision and talents of these individuals, and perhaps a few others, to capture the chaos and despair of the modern age for posterity. They summoned the strength to stare down a brutally violent time and hold a mirror up to it, so that perhaps future generations would not be destined to repeat our most profoundly tragic mistakes.

CHRONOLOGY

1881	Born Pablo Ruiz Picasso in Málaga, Spain, on October 25
1891	Family moves to La Coruña in northwest Spain
1892	Picasso begins formal art training at the Da Guarda Institute in La Coruña
1895	Picasso's sister Conchita dies; family moves to Barcelona, where Picasso enrolls at the Llotja
1897	Picasso enrolls in Madrid's Royal Academy of San Fernando; wins gold medal for his painting *Science and Charity* at the Málaga Provincial Exhibition
1898	Treaty of Paris signed by Spain, ending the Spanish-American War; Spain plunges into economic depression
1899	Picasso returns to Barcelona, drops out of the Llotja, and leads a bohemian life
1900	Exhibits work at Els Quatre Gats café; visits Paris for the first time
1901–4	Has first major exhibit in Paris, which brings him to the attention of the art world; begins to paint more somber canvases—including *Child Holding a Dove, Two Saltimbanques,* and *The Old Guitarist*—that are later grouped together as the blue period
1904	Settles permanently in Paris and moves into Le Bateau Lavoir; meets Fernande Olivier; rose period begins as Picasso's paintings, many of circus performers, take on a brighter hue

1906	Becomes interested in African art, which influences his portrait of Gertrude Stein
1907	Paints *Les Demoiselles d'Avignon,* creating a revolution in 20th-century art; meets Georges Braque, with whom he invents cubism
1910	Picasso's paintings are exhibited in England, Germany, and Hungary
1911	Picasso has first exhibition in New York, where most critics attack his work; ends his seven-year relationship with Olivier
1912	Begins to achieve international recognition; experiments with synthetic cubism; creates *Still Life with Chair Caning,* the world's first collage
1914–18	Declines to fight in World War I and spends war years in Paris; collaborates on the controversial ballet *Parade*; marries Olga Kokhlova
1920s	A major figure in the international art world, Picasso delves into surrealism and sculpture
1921	Son, Paulo, is born
1927	"Thirty Years of Pablo Picasso," a major exhibition, opens in London
1935	Daughter, María de la Concepción, is born to Picasso and Marie-Thérèse Walter
1936	Spanish Civil War begins; Picasso is among artists represented in the Museum of Modern Art's exhibition "Cubism and Abstract Art"
1937	Fascists bomb the city of Guernica; in protest, Picasso paints *Guernica* mural for the Spanish Pavilion at the Paris World's Fair
1939–40	Fascists triumph in Spain; World War II begins; Picasso remains in Paris under German occupation

1944	Picasso's play *Desire Caught by the Tail* is staged by leading French artists
1945	As World War II ends, Picasso joins the Communist party; paints many antiwar canvases
1947	Son, Claude, is born to Picasso and Françoise Gilot
1948	Picasso moves to Vallauris and revitalizes the town's ceramics industry
1949	Daughter, Paloma, is born
1950	Picasso attends the Second World Peace Conference in Sheffield, England; is awarded the Lenin Peace Prize
1957	Major U.S. exhibition marks Picasso's 75th birthday
1961	Marries Jacqueline Roque; moves into new villa near Mougins, France
1962	Museum of Modern Art mounts a major exhibition in honor of Picasso's 80th birthday
1963	Museo Picasso opens in Barcelona
1966	Major Picasso exhibition in Paris organized under the auspices of French minister for cultural affairs André Malraux; paintings begin to sell at record prices
1971	Picasso named honorary citizen of Paris; worldwide observances mark his 90th birthday
1972	"Picasso in the Collection of the Museum of Modern Art" opens in New York
1973	Picasso dies at Mougins on April 8

FURTHER READING

Arnheim, Rudolf. *The Genesis of a Painting: Picasso's Guernica.* Berkeley: University of California Press, 1980.

Barr, Alfred H., Jr. *Picasso: Fifty Years of His Art.* New York: Museum of Modern Art, 1974.

Cabanne, Pierre. *Pablo Picasso: His Life and Times.* Translated by Harold J. Salemson. New York: Morrow, 1977.

Duncan, David Douglas. *Goodbye Picasso.* New York: Grosset & Dunlap, 1974.

Gallwitz, Klaus. *Picasso at 90: The Late Work.* New York: Putnam, 1971.

Gilot, Françoise. *Life with Picasso.* New York: Avon, 1981.

Homage to Pablo Picasso. Edited by Gualtieri di San Lazzaro. Translated by Bettina Wadia. New York: Tudor Publishing Company, 1971.

La Farge, Ann. *Gertrude Stein.* New York: Chelsea House Publishers, 1988.

Olivier, Fernande. *Picasso and His Friends.* Translated by Jane Miller. New York: Appleton–Century, 1965.

Otero, Roberto. *Forever Picasso: An Intimate Look at His Last Years.* Translated by Elaine Kerrigan. New York: Abrams, 1974.

Penrose, Roland. *Picasso: His Life and Work.* Berkeley: University of California Press, 1981.

Porzio, Domenico, and Marco Valsecchi. *Understanding Picasso.* New York: Newsweek Books, 1973.

Ramie, Georges. *Picasso's Ceramics.* Translated by Kenneth Lyons. New York: Viking, 1976.

Richardson, John. *A Life of Picasso: Volume I, 1881–1906.* New York: Random House, 1991.

Rubin, William, ed. *Pablo Picasso: A Retrospective.* New York: Museum of Modern Art, 1980.

Spies, Werner. *Picasso's Complete Sculpture.* San Francisco: Alan Wofsy Fine Arts, 1988.

Sutton, Denys. *The Complete Paintings of Picasso (Blue & Rose Period).* New York: Penguin, 1987.

Tinterow, Gary. *Master Drawings by Picasso.* New York: Braziller, 1981.

Walther, Ingo F. *Picasso: Genius of the Century.* New York: Parkwest Publications, 1987.

Wertenbaker, Lael Tucker. *The World of Picasso.* Rev. ed. New York: Time-Life Books, 1980.

INDEX

JOHN W. SELFRIDGE is a New York–based writer and editor with a special interest in 20th-century history and culture. He holds an M.A. from Columbia University Teachers College, a J.D. from Rutgers Law School, and is currently editorial director at a major educational publishing house. He has written four biographies for middle school readers, including *Mikhail Gorbachev* in the Chelsea House series JUNIOR WORLD BIOGRAPHIES.

RODOLFO CARDONA is professor of Spanish and comparative literature at Boston University. A renowned scholar, he has written many works of criticism, including *Ramón, a Study of Gómez de la Serna and His Works and Visión del esperpento: Teoría y práctica del esperpento en Valle-Inclán*. Born in San José, Costa Rica, he earned his B.A. and M.A. from Louisiana State University and received a Ph.D. from the University of Washington. He has taught at Case Western Reserve University, the University of Pittsburgh, the University of Texas at Austin, the University of New Mexico, and Harvard University.

JAMES COCKCROFT is currently a visiting professor of Latin American and Caribbean studies at the State University of New York at Albany. A three-time Fulbright scholar, he earned a Ph.D. from Stanford University and has taught at the University of Massachusetts, the University of Vermont, and the University of Connecticut. He is the author or coauthor of numerous books on Latin American subjects, including *Neighbors in Turmoil: Latin America, The Hispanic Experience in the United States: Contemporary Issues and Perspectives,* and *Outlaws in the Promised Land: Mexican Immigrant Workers and America's Future.*